2025 CHRISTMAS
with Southern Living

INSPIRED IDEAS FOR HOLIDAY
COOKING & DECORATING

2025
CHRISTMAS
with Southern Living

INSPIRED IDEAS FOR HOLIDAY
COOKING & DECORATING

Southern Living BOOKS

CONTENTS

WELCOME LETTER 9

DECORATE 10
ENTERTAIN 54
SAVOR 104
SHARE 156

RESOURCES 168
GENERAL INDEX 170
METRIC CHARTS 172
RECIPE INDEX 173
HOLIDAY PLANNER 177

A LITTLE CHRISTMAS, PAGE 28

SERVE UP GOOD
CHEER MENU,
PAGE 57

Soon after jack-o'-lanterns disappear from porches and autumn leaves begin to fall, the holiday season is upon us. Whether you're a deck-the-halls-the-week-of-Thanksgiving type or prefer to wait until mid-December to bring the ornaments down from the attic, tradition reigns supreme this time of year. Seeing how family and friends celebrate and decorate is always fun.

This 2025 edition of *Christmas with Southern Living* provides a glimpse inside a multigenerational family home, including pictures of how the house looked during the holidays in the middle of the last century and how the original owners' granddaughter has updated it in a kaleidoscope of juicy color today.

Another couple, the Littles, built a backyard shed that is anything but utilitarian. Like a bespoke playhouse for grown-ups draped in holiday finery for Christmastime, it's where their friends and family gather while the kids play outside or in the main house. If you need "A Little Christmas" right this very minute, their shed is proof that you can create something magical just about anywhere.

Feeling crafty? We show you how to create inviting holiday vignettes using citrus, apples, and pears mixed with spices, greenery, and flowers. The decorations may be fleeting, but the bold displays are timeless.

If you're craving connection over sips and nibbles, we've got ideas for entertaining covered, from cocktail hour and a formal holiday dinner to a dessert party and New Year's good-luck feast. Of course, the classic cookbook section is packed with starters, sides, main courses, and desserts that may be mixed and matched to create delicious menus of your own.

Never let the hustle and bustle of this busy time of year overwhelm you. Tackle your to-do list head-on with our helpful Holiday Planner, which will guide you every step of the way so you can mix, mingle, and enjoy this special time of year from start to finish.

Merry Christmas!

Katherine Cobbs
EDITOR

DECORATE
holiday lookbook

Kaleidoscope Christmas

A new generation gives a beloved family home a fresh, vibrant update just in time to gather for the joyful holiday season. A passed-down scrapbook of "before" photos highlights the home's original, understated decor. In contrast, the new "after" photos prove that great design and classic pieces can be bold, and that the most striking holiday displays are often anything but traditional red and green.

Juicy holiday hues add a whimsical touch to a lush centerpiece, which rises from an ironstone tureen on the table in the bright breakfast nook. The arrangement features roses, peonies, and anemones in shades of magenta, raspberry, periwinkle, and coral, combined with delicate longleaf pine branches and green hellebores, creating a striking Christmas display beneath a sparkling crystal chandelier. A trio of wreaths, each adorned with satin bows that echo the colors of the chintz drapery, beautifully dresses up the windows and complements the layered patterns on the banquette.

DECORATE

Pink and green steal the scene in the dining room, where what was old is new again. The updated space exemplifies how classic architecture stands the test of time. Modern updates enhance the space's aesthetics for the 21st century. The blushing floral wallpaper draws inspiration from the room's original walls but in a palette that adds a lively touch. White dining chairs upholstered in apple green and a white marble-topped sideboard brighten the space and create a striking contrast against the dark, rich wood finishes. A contemporary chandelier adds festive sparkle above the table, reminiscent of champagne bubbles.

DECORATE

A low centerpiece of acid green moss and pink hypericum makes conversation easy, while the translucent, handblown glass trees keep this holiday look light and airy. Wicker bells at each place setting mimic the large wicker urns adorned with paper flowers and add textural interest.

The homeowner's collection of heirloom Pink Cockatrice plates is a pretty backdrop for a lush display of pink pepperberry, celadon hellebores, and ranunculus blooms in sorbet colors.

DECORATE

The round pedestal dining table encourages conversation and feels less formal than the grandparents' expansive rectangular table in the "before" photo on *page 16*. Hidden leaves allow the new table to expand to accommodate additional guests.

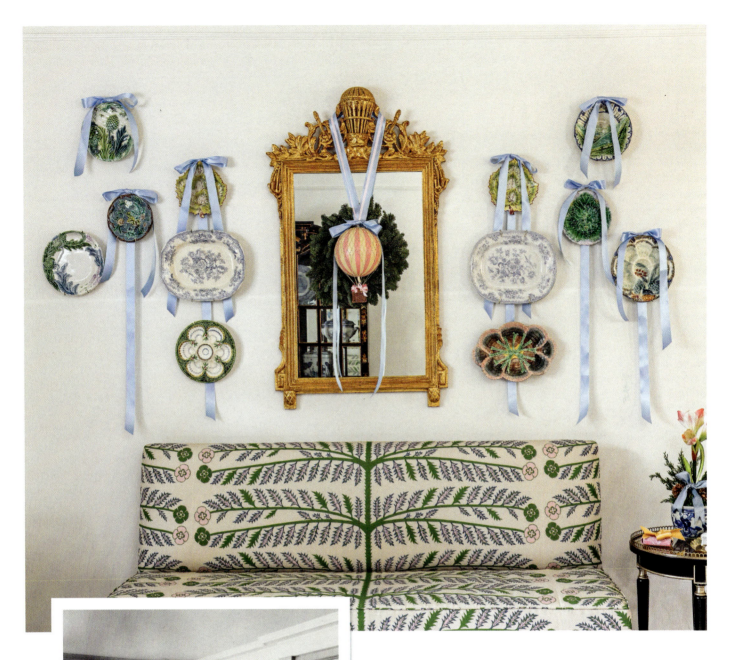

Today, the living room feels lighter and brighter without heavy drapery and dark wallpaper, while the original features, such as the woodwork, moldings, and pink marble fireplace surround, remain intact. A delicate asparagus fern enhances a new mantelpiece with simpler carved details. Repeating shades of green and cream, with a pop of lavender in gifts tucked into stockings, keeps the mantel display simple. Across the room, plates and platters adorned with waterfalls of satin ribbon flank a gilt mirror above a pretty settee upholstered in Schumacher Thistle fabric. The hot air balloon ornament repeats the mirror's carved top.

DECORATE

"*Your bright green leaves with festive cheer Give hope and strength throughout the year*"

—'O CHRISTMAS TREE' LYRIC

A towering fir tree in the windows facing the front yard serves as the focal point of the living room this time of year, much like the heavily flocked tree did during Christmases past. The homeowners' love of color is expressed here with bright ornaments, glittering garlands, and vibrant bows. Beneath the tree, a rainbow of colorful packages continues the cheerful theme.

DECORATE

23

The light-drenched sunroom that opens to the pool in the backyard is a place the family flocks to throughout the year. Its mix of pastel and bright Easter-egg hues gets the Christmas treatment with greenery-topped trays, a fuchsia poinsettia planted in a chinoiserie bowl, and purple anemones mixed with plumosa, pine, and eucalyptus in a cut crystal compote.

DECORATE

Chandeliers with crystal petals conjure icy snowflakes this time of year.

The grounds surrounding the home have also undergone a modern metamorphosis, though garden elements like statuary remain to greet guests. This time of year, a statue of St. Francis of Assisi, patron saint of animals and ecology, opposite, is cloaked in ribbon and a wreath of greenery. In the courtyard, draped in cypress and pepper berry, a 1958 bronze rendering of the Four Seasons, above, by sculptor Leonard D. McMurry is dressed for winter.

DECORATE

27

A Little Christmas

Get inspired to make any space magical.
At Christmastime, Sarah Kate and Jason Little's
garden shed morphs into an enchanting
holiday escape where friends and family
can mix, mingle, and make lasting memories
during this most festive season.

Waves of garland strung from the room's center to its corners form a canopy of green overhead to create a woodland escape.

"For we need a little music,
need a little laughter"

'WE NEED A LITTLE CHRISTMAS' LYRIC

Throughout the year, the Littles' garden shed is a welcome escape where the couple comes to read, write letters, listen to albums on the record player, and relax with friends while their children play outside. Decking this little gathering place as they would their home makes sense. Only here, the decor takes a cue from the shed's garden surroundings, relying heavily on clippings from the yard's trees and shrubs mixed with flowers, ornaments, garden elements, and collected objects.

DECORATE

Another way to bring the outdoors in with holiday flair is to use gilded natural accents. The garlands are made by tracing fallen leaves and bird and flower shapes on gold foil sheets and stringing them together with gold thread. Acorns and seed pods are gilded with spray paint to create shimmering ornaments or natural vase fillers. Both crafts achieve an elevated organic look that picks up on the brass and gold elements in the furnishings and accessories throughout the room.

A writing desk serves as a gift-wrapping station, complete with gift tags, toppers, ribbons, and beautiful wrapping paper. All who visit the shed can enjoy the collection of French vase de mariée, or wedding vases, filled with pretty posies until each goes to its lucky recipient. Choosing one unique item as your signature gift simplifies holiday giving.

DECORATE

37

Much like a secret garden oasis hidden behind dense hedgerows, the Littles' quaint backyard outbuilding only appears to be a place for composting and potting plants. The surprise and delight happens when guests enter to find a bespoke holiday hideaway that offers all the comforts of a fine home. The Louis XVI sideboard houses both a record collection and turntable as well as spirits and mixers for impromptu cocktail-hour gatherings. The 10-foot sofa, designed by Steven Gambrel, was an auction find that accommodates large crowds in the small space. For major impact on the shed's periwinkle walls, a beloved oil painting was scanned, enlarged, and cropped into multiple sections. Each section was then printed on canvas and framed for a bold display *(pages 30-31)*. All of these things together prove that good interior design doesn't require major square footage, and no matter the size, rooms with a collected, layered look are the most inviting. We all need a Little Christmas, right this very minute!

Festive Fruits

The holidays can be hectic and expensive, but decorating shouldn't be. Beyond the boxes of cherished ornaments and yards of string lights, enlist the everyday items you already have and then add a little embellishment with greenery, fresh fruit, and spices. It's a great way to tickle that creative muscle and create something beautiful without breaking the bank.

Citrus are abundant in winter. These cool-season fruits are an excellent material for decking the halls. Use oranges, lemons, and limes to create eye-catching displays, whether sliced and dried in a low oven, left whole, or studded with cloves. Here, dried orange slices add color to an evergreen wreath. Drying the fruit slices helps them last throughout the season. On the sideboard, whole clementines are attached to a foam sphere with picks, creating a striking, fragrant topiary that rises from a sterling silver bowl lined with moss. Clusters of wax flowers and hypericum berries fill gaps and camouflage the foam. Placing more whole fruit atop the graceful curve of an evergreen garland adds more no-fuss interest to this focal point.

A chest in the living room by the Christmas tree and roaring fire is ideal for serving cocktails or after-dinner drinks. On the table, fresh fruit is studded with cloves, a natural preservative, and mixed with dried slices and greenery for a fresh centerpiece and setting. Dry sliced and whole citrus on racks set over sheet pans in a low oven. Citrus slices take about 8 to 10 hours to dry completely, while whole fruit is best slit and oven-dried at least 24 hours. A dedicated food dehydrator makes quicker work of the process. To preserve dried fruit for future seasons and lock in the color, place the dried fruit in a paper bag filled with orris root powder (available online) for 1 week before dusting off to store, wrapped in tissue paper, in a cool, dark place.

DECORATE

Apples of all varieties and colors— green Granny Smith, yellow Golden Delicious, or blushing Pink Lady—are striking accents to weave into holiday tableaus. Small, sunset-hued Lady Apples play well with the towering red amaryllis in the foyer and pick up on the rich, russet veining of an antique mahogany box. Using more apples as the "mulch" for a lemon cypress tree and mixed in with wrapped packages, bottle brush trees, and garland proves that the most striking displays are often the simplest.

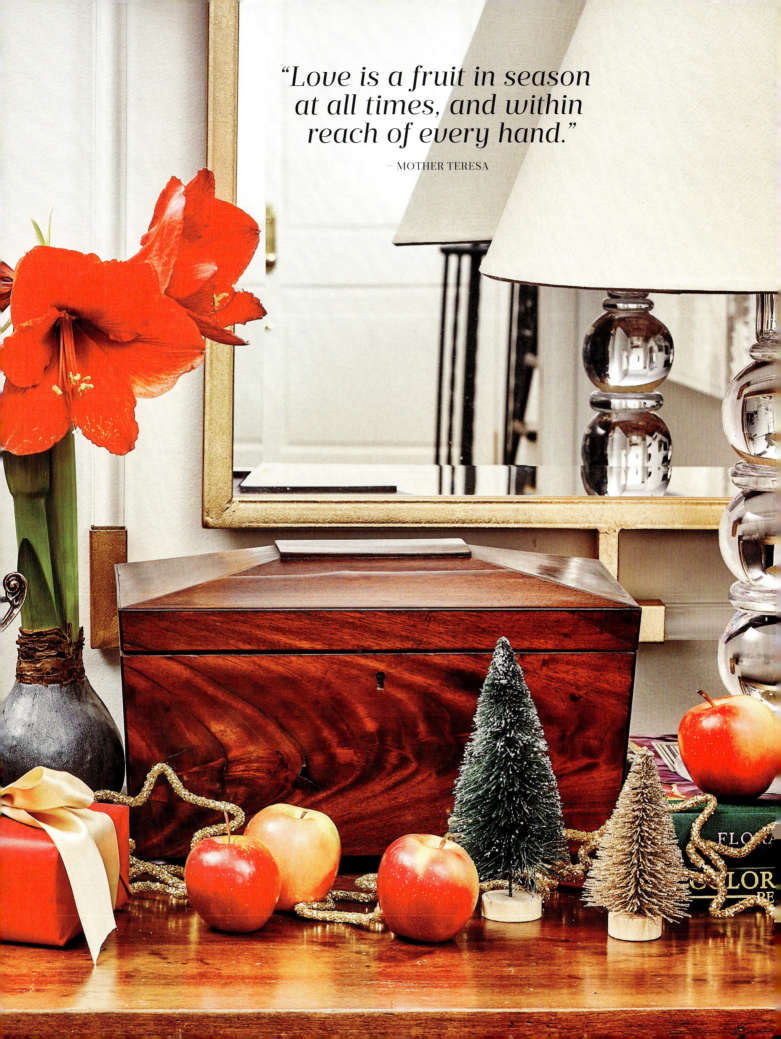

"Love is a fruit in season at all times, and within reach of every hand."

— MOTHER TERESA

A faux wreath serves as the form to build out this inviting medley of fresh greenery, berries, and apples mixed with dried apple slices, eucalyptus, and pine cones. A plaid taffeta ribbon picks up on the array of colorful materials used. Many of those same elements in dried form create a pretty fruit-and-spice potpourri that is as great for giving as it is for filling bowls throughout the house.

DECORATE

Like apples, pears are another autumn fruit that can be enlisted into service when it's time to deck the halls. Choose rustic brown Bosc, red or green D'Anjou, red or golden Bartlett, blushing-gold Comice, towering green Concorde, or diminutive Forelle or Seckel pears. Small red D'Anjou pears make a pretty, edible holder for place cards atop Christmas china on the dining room table. Historically, fresh fruit was considered a rare treat during wintertime, so giving the fruit at Christmas was a sign of generosity and sharing in the season's abundant joy.

Using a glue gun to secure a star anise pod to the tops of dried pear slices with their tree-form shape turns them into homespun Christmas tree ornaments that scream "fa la la la la!" A mix of fresh bosc pears and faux miniature green pears come together to create a towering topiary in the kitchen. Blushing pepper berries with their pointed leaves fill the spaces between the fruit and add festive embellishment that is repeated in the bud vases holding fragrant paperwhites and fernlike cypress stems.

DECORATE

ENTERTAIN

holiday menus

Serve Up Good Cheer

Even hosts will be happy with this festive cocktail party menu that comes together in a flash.

menu

Grapefruit, Rosemary, and Sage Sparkler
Mini Beef Wellingtons
Smoked Salmon Mousse Canapés
Cheesy Caramelized Onion Flatbreads
Okra in a Blanket
Bourbon-Chocolate Baby Bombes

ENTERTAIN

Grapefruit, Rosemary, and Sage Sparkler

SERVES **1**
ACTIVE **5 MIN.**
TOTAL **5 MIN.**

Winter flavors of citrus and woodsy herbs add heady flavor to this holiday spritzer.

Grapefruit wedge and sparkling sugar for rimming (optional)
3 large fresh sage leaves
1 small fresh rosemary sprig
2 tsp. granulated sugar
3 Tbsp. (1½ oz.) freshly squeezed grapefruit juice
3 Tbsp. (1½ oz.) dry gin
3 Tbsp. (1½ oz.) chilled dry champagne or sparkling wine
Grapefruit peel spiral, for garnish
Rosemary sprig, for garnish

1. Run a grapefruit wedge around the edge of the glass, then dip the rim in sparkling sugar to coat, if desired.

2. Combine sage, rosemary, and sugar in a cocktail shaker. Muddle herbs to release their flavor. Fill shaker with grapefruit juice, gin, and 1 cup ice. Cover and shake vigorously about 20 seconds or until well chilled. Strain into a chilled cocktail glass or champagne flute. Top with champagne, and stir gently. Garnish with grapefruit spiral and additional rosemary sprig.

MAKE IT A MOCKTAIL

Substitute 3 Tbsp. (1½ oz.) additional grapefruit juice for the gin and chilled sparkling white grape juice for the dry champagne or sparkling wine.

MINI BEEF WELLINGTONS

OKRA IN A BLANKET

MINI BEEF WELLINGTONS

CHEESY CARAMELIZED ONION FLATBREADS

OKRA IN A BLANKET

SMOKED SALMON MOUSSE CANAPÉS

Mini Beef Wellingtons

SERVES **8 TO 10**
ACTIVE **25 MIN.**
TOTAL **45 MIN., INCLUDING STANDING**

Guests will love this downsized take on the showstopping beef Wellington—they are filling and easily eaten out of hand while mixing and mingling.

- 1 Tbsp. extra-virgin olive oil
- 4 to 5 cremini mushrooms or button mushrooms, sliced
- ½ tsp. finely chopped fresh rosemary
- ½ tsp. finely chopped fresh thyme
- ¼ tsp. black pepper
- Sea salt
- 1 large egg, lightly beaten
- 1 (17.3-oz.) pkg. frozen puff pastry dough (2 sheets), thawed
- 1 (1-lb.) trimmed beef tenderloin, cut into 24 cubes (about ¾ inch each)
- ⅓ cup Boursin cheese, such as Caramelized Onion and Herb

1. Preheat oven to 450°F. Heat oil in a medium nonstick skillet over medium. Add mushrooms and herbs; cook until browned, 3 minutes. Stir in pepper and ⅛ teaspoon sea salt. Set aside.

2. Whisk together egg and 1 tablespoon water in a small bowl.

3. Roll 1 puff pastry sheet into a 9-x-12-inch rectangle on a lightly floured work surface. Cut into 12 (3-inch) squares. Arrange 1 beef cube in the center of each pastry square, and sprinkle with a pinch of sea salt. Top each beef cube with about ½ teaspoon Boursin cheese and 1 mushroom slice. Brush edges of pastry squares with egg mixture. Fold dough corners over filling in the center to make a packet, pinching to seal. Place on a large, parchment paper–lined baking sheet. Repeat with remaining ingredients, and brush all with remaining egg mixture.

4. Bake in preheated oven until pastry if puffed and golden brown, 14 to 16 minutes. Let stand 5 minutes before serving.

Smoked Salmon Mousse Canapés

SERVES **8 TO 10**
ACTIVE **15 MIN.**
TOTAL **15 MIN.**

This light bite is elegant and super simple to make. The salmon mousse is also delicious spooned into hollowed-out cooked new potato halves for a heartier nibble.

- 8 oz. hot- or cold-smoked salmon
- 1 (8-oz.) pkg. cream cheese
- 3 Tbsp. half-and-half
- 2 tsp. fresh lemon juice
- ¼ tsp. sea salt
- ¼ tsp. black pepper
- 1 Tbsp. finely chopped fresh tarragon
- 1 large English cucumber, cut into 30 (⅓-inch-thick) slices, or 30 small whole grain crackers
- Caviar, for garnish
- Chopped fresh chives, for garnish

1. Place salmon in a food processor; pulse until finely chopped. Add cream cheese, half-and-half, lemon juice, salt, and pepper and process until creamy and fluffy. Add tarragon; pulse until evenly combined. Taste and adjust seasoning, if necessary. (Note: Add more half-and-half if necessary to achieve the desired texture for piping.)

2. Pipe or dollop about 1 tablespoon salmon mousse onto each cucumber slice. Garnish with caviar and chives.

Cheesy Caramelized Onion Flatbreads

SERVES **8**
ACTIVE **15 MIN.**
TOTAL **45 MIN., INCLUDING STANDING**

Ooey, gooey, cheese-topped anything is a guaranteed crowd-pleaser, and this herbaceous, flavorful flatbread is no exception.

- 2 Tbsp. extra virgin olive oil, divided
- ½ large white onion, very thinly sliced
- ¼ tsp. kosher salt, divided
- 2 soft flatbreads or naan (about 4 to 5 oz. each)
- ½ cup fresh ricotta cheese
- 1 large garlic clove, minced
- 4 oz. fresh mozzarella cheese, thinly sliced (about 6 slices)
- ¼ cup freshly grated Pecorino Romano cheese
- ¾ tsp. black sesame seeds
- 1 Tbsp. thinly sliced fresh basil
- 1 Tbsp. thinly sliced fresh mint
- 1 tsp. orange zest

1. Preheat oven to 450°F. Heat 1½ tablespoons oil in a nonstick skillet over medium-high heat. Add onion and ⅛ teaspoon salt; cook until onion slices are lightly caramelized, about 8 minutes. Transfer to a small bowl.

2. Brush flatbreads with remaining 1½ teaspoons oil. Stir together ricotta, garlic, and remaining ⅛ teaspoon salt in a small mixing bowl, and spread onto flatbreads. Top evenly with mozzarella, Pecorino Romano, and caramelized onion. Sprinkle with sesame seeds.

3. Place flatbreads on a large baking sheet, and bake in preheated oven until cheese is melted and flatbreads are crisp, about 12 minutes. Let stand 5 minutes. Sprinkle with basil, mint, and orange zest, and cut into slices.

Okra in a Blanket

SERVES **12 TO 14**
ACTIVE **20 MIN.**
TOTAL **20 MIN.**

This fun take on pigs in a blanket shakes things up by wrapping a Southern favorite—pickled okra—in a blanket of thinly sliced country ham. A mustard-forward dipping sauce is a delicious dunk for these skewered two-bite appetizers.

- ½ cup mayonnaise
- 2 Tbsp. Dijon mustard
- 4 tsp. honey
- 1 tsp. chopped fresh dill
- ⅛ tsp. kosher salt
- 30 whole pickled okra pods (from 1 [64-oz.] jar)
- 4 thin slices country ham, cut into ½-inch-wide strips

Whisk together mayonnaise, Dijon mustard, honey, fresh dill, and kosher salt in a small bowl until well combined. Line a baking sheet with paper towels; place pickled okra on baking sheet to drain. Wrap 1 ham strip around each okra pod, securing with a wooden pick. Transfer wrapped okra to a large platter. Serve with mustard sauce.

ENTERTAIN

Bourbon-Chocolate Baby Bombes

SERVES 12 • ACTIVE 35 MIN. • TOTAL 1 HOUR, PLUS 1 HOUR COOLING AND CHILLING

This one is for the chocolate lovers. The cake is light, tender, and moist with a rich chocolaty flavor. The addition of cold-brew concentrate intensifies the chocolate flavor. Each baby bombe is cloaked in bittersweet chocolate, giving these decadent morsels a truffle-esque quality. (If you wish to skip the alcohol, just add vanilla to taste.) The toasted pecan garnish adds welcome crunch.

CAKES

Baking spray

1 cup all-purpose flour

¾ cup granulated sugar

¼ cup packed light brown sugar

¼ cup unsweetened cocoa, sifted

1 tsp. baking soda

½ tsp. baking powder

½ tsp. kosher salt

1 large egg, at room temperature

¼ cup sour cream, at room temperature

¼ cup vegetable oil

¼ cup bottled cold-brew coffee concentrate, at room temperature

½ tsp. vanilla extract

½ tsp. bourbon

½ cup hot water

BOURBON GANACHE

2 (4-oz.) 60% cacao bittersweet chocolate bars (such as Ghirardelli), finely chopped

½ cup heavy whipping cream

1 Tbsp. light corn syrup

2 Tbsp. bourbon

Chopped toasted pecans

1. Prepare the Cakes: Preheat oven to 350°F. Coat a 12-cup muffin tray with baking spray. Line bottom of each well with a round of parchment paper; set aside.

2. Whisk together flour, granulated sugar, brown sugar, cocoa, baking soda, baking powder, and salt in a large bowl. Whisk together egg, sour cream, oil, coffee concentrate, vanilla, and bourbon in a medium bowl. Add egg mixture to flour mixture; whisk just until combined. Add hot water, whisking until combined and mostly smooth.

3. Divide batter among prepared wells. Bake in preheated oven until a wooden pick inserted in center comes out clean, 12 to 15 minutes. Let cool in tray on a wire rack 5 minutes; remove Cakes from pan and place upright on wire rack. Remove and discard parchment paper. Let cool completely, 30 to 45 minutes.

4. Prepare the Bourbon Ganache: When Cakes are cool, add water to a medium saucepan, filling to a depth of 1 inch. Bring to a boil over medium-high; reduce heat to medium-low, and simmer. Place chocolate, cream, and corn syrup in a medium heatproof bowl; place over simmering water in pan. (Make sure bottom of bowl does not touch water.) Cook over medium-low, stirring occasionally and adjusting heat as needed to maintain a simmer, until chocolate mixture is melted and smooth, 4 to 5 minutes. Remove from heat; whisk in bourbon until smooth and combined.

5. Place Cakes on wire rack over a parchment paper-lined baking sheet. Spoon enough Bourbon Ganache over 1 cooled Cake to coat as desired; repeat with remaining Cakes and Bourbon Ganache. Garnish tops with pecans. Chill until ganache is set, about 30 minutes.

Pro Tip:
GANACHE SUCCESS

Your ganache should be able to easily drizzle from the spoon in order to coat your cakes evenly. If you find it's gotten thicker than you'd like, you can microwave it on HIGH in 10- to 15-second intervals, stirring between each until it loosens back up.

ENTERTAIN

Relish the Feast

From appetizer to dessert, a special relish, topping, or garnish makes each dish holiday special.

menu

Paper Plane Cocktail
The Southern Relish Tray: Zesty Pickled Roots,
Warm Olives with Citrus Zest, Pickled Beets,
Roquefort-Cognac Cheese Spread
Pomegranate, Pear, and Arugula Salad
Mulled Cider-Cranberry Relish
Green Beans with Garlic Vinaigrette
Two-Potato Gratin
Dry-Brined Turkey with Pecan Gremolata
Vanilla Layer Cake with Fruit-and-Herb Wreath

ENTERTAIN

Paper Plane Cocktail

SERVES **1**
ACTIVE **5 MIN.**
TOTAL **5 MIN.**

A paper plane cocktail is disarmingly delicious, perfectly well balanced, and bright, with vanilla sweetness from the bourbon and bitter citrus from the Aperol and Amaro Nonino. The usual mix for a paper plane is one part each of the alcohols and one part lemon juice. Our recipe uses slightly different proportions, going heavier on the bourbon so it's ever-so-slightly more Southern.

3 Tbsp. (1½ oz.) bourbon (over 90 proof)
2 Tbsp. (1 oz.) Amaro Nonino Quintessentia
2 Tbsp. (1 oz.) Aperol
1 Tbsp. (½ oz.) fresh lemon juice (from 1 lemon)
¼ tsp. simple syrup
Dehydrated blood orange or navel orange slice, for garnish
Paper plane and cocktail skewer, for garnish (optional)

1. Combine bourbon, Amaro Nonino Quintessentia, Aperol, lemon juice, and simple syrup in a cocktail shaker; fill shaker with ice. Cover tightly with lid, and shake until blended and chilled, about 30 seconds. Strain into a 6-ounce coupe glass.

2. Garnish with 1 dehydrated blood orange or navel orange slice. If desired, thread a paper plane onto a cocktail skewer, and place in glass; serve immediately.

SUBLIME SUBSTITUTES

Amaro swap: If Amaro Nonino Quintessentia is hard to find, Amaro Montenegro can be used instead.

Sweeten up: The simple syrup is optional in this drink. Go without if you like a more bitter cocktail, or keep it in for a sweeter cocktail.

On the side: Beside the dehydrated orange peel garnish, the paper plane is an optional garnish. Leave it off if two large garnishes feels too fussy for your taste.

SOUTHERN RELISH TRAY

The Southern Relish Tray

SERVES **10** • ACTIVE **10 MIN.** • TOTAL **4 HOURS, 10 MIN.**

The start of many Southern feasts is a palate-priming relish tray that whets the appetite for the meal to come. A great one offers a medley of brined and pickled things mixed with a little something creamy and something crunchy for flavorful balance.

Zesty Pickled Roots

SERVES **10**
ACTIVE **10 MIN.**
TOTAL **4 HOURS, 10 MIN.**

Sweet heat amps up the flavor of these jewel-tone carrots.

- 1 lb. small root vegetables, such as carrots, parsnips, turnips, or radishes, tops trimmed to ½ inch
- 1½ cups white vinegar
- 1 cup water
- ¼ cup granulated sugar
- 1½ tsp. kosher salt
- 1 tsp. onion powder
- 1 tsp. crushed red pepper
- ½ tsp. mustard seeds

1. Place desired root vegetables in a medium saucepan with water to cover, and bring to a boil over high. Reduce heat to medium, and simmer just until tender, 8 to 10 minutes. Drain and rinse with cold water; drain completely, and place in a large bowl.

2. Stir together vinegar, water, sugar, salt, onion powder, crushed red pepper, and mustard seeds in a medium saucepan. Bring to a boil over medium-high, stirring to dissolve sugar and salt. Pour hot liquid over carrots; cover and chill at least 4 hours or up to overnight.

Warm Olives with Citrus Zest

MAKES **ABOUT 2 CUPS**
ACTIVE **10 MIN.**
TOTAL **16 MIN.**

Swap the charcuterie for meaty brined olives served warm.

- ¼ cup extra-virgin olive oil
- ¼ tsp. fennel seeds
- 1 tsp. coriander seeds
- 1 cup Kalamata olives
- 1 cup Castelvetrano olives
- 1 bay leaf
- 1 wide strip lemon zest, julienned
- 1 wide strip orange zest, julienned
- 3 pinches dried red pepper flakes

Heat oil in a skillet over medium. Add fennel and coriander seeds; cook, stirring occasionally, until fragrant, 3 minutes. Add olives, bay leaf, citrus zest, red pepper flakes, and ¼ cup water. Cook, stirring occasionally, until heated through, about 3 minutes. Serve warm.

Pickled Beets

SERVES **10**
ACTIVE **20 MIN.**
TOTAL **5 HOURS**

Pickling tames the inherent earthiness of beets.

- 1½ lb. small red beets
- 1 cup apple cider vinegar
- 1 cup water
- ½ cup granulated sugar
- ½ cup thinly sliced red onion
- 2 tsp. dried thyme
- 1 tsp. dried oregano
- 1 tsp. kosher salt
- 1 tsp. black peppercorns

1. Trim ends of beets, leaving roots and 1-inch stems; scrub with a brush. Place in a medium saucepan with water to cover; bring to a boil over high. Cover, reduce heat to medium, and simmer until tender, about 45 minutes. Drain and rinse with cold water, and drain completely. Cool 5 minutes. Trim roots, and rub off skins.

2. Cut beets into ¼-inch-thick slices, and place in a large bowl. Stir together apple cider vinegar, water, sugar, red onion, thyme, oregano, kosher salt, and black peppercorns in a medium saucepan. Bring to a boil over medium-high, stirring to dissolve sugar and salt. Pour hot liquid over beets; cover and chill at least 4 hours or up to overnight.

Roquefort-Cognac Cheese Spread

MAKES **ABOUT 1¼ CUPS**
ACTIVE **10 MIN.**
TOTAL **2 HOURS, 10 MIN.**

Inspired by a recipe from Julia Child, this sharp, tangy spread elevates the humble celery stick or cracker into an unforgettable appetizer.

- ½ (8-oz.) pkg. cream cheese, softened
- ¼ cup butter, softened
- 4 oz. Roquefort or other blue cheese, crumbled
- 1½ Tbsp. minced fresh chives
- 1 Tbsp. minced celery
- 1 Tbsp. Cognac
- ⅛ tsp. cayenne pepper
- ⅛ tsp. black pepper
- Celery sticks

1. Combine cream cheese and butter in a medium bowl. Beat with an electric mixer on medium with until smooth. Beat in blue cheese, chives, minced celery, Cognac, cayenne, and black pepper on low speed until blended.

2. Spoon into a serving bowl. Chill 2 hours. Spoon spread into celery sticks to serve. If you like, garnish with additional chives.

Pomegranate, Pear, and Arugula Salad

SERVES **8**
ACTIVE **10 MIN.**
TOTAL **10 MIN.**

This refreshing salad adds a dose of holiday color to every place setting.

DRESSING
½ cup fresh orange juice
¼ cup fresh lemon juice
½ tsp. kosher salt
⅛ tsp. black pepper
⅛ tsp. paprika
1 shallot, finely chopped
1 garlic clove, crushed
1 tsp. Dijon mustard
⅓ cup olive oil

SALAD
6 cups baby arugula
2 pears, quartered, cored, cut into ¼-inch-thick slices
1 cup pomegranate seeds

1. Whisk together orange juice, lemon juice, salt, pepper, paprika, shallot, garlic, and mustard in a large bowl. Whisk in oil.

2. Add arugula, pears, and pomegranate seeds to the bowl; toss and serve immediately.

Mulled Cider–Cranberry Relish

SERVES **8**
ACTIVE **5 MIN.**
TOTAL **30 MIN.**

Warm spices and apples add traditional flavor to this classic holiday relish.

12 oz. fresh or frozen cranberries
1 Tbsp. orange zest
1½ cups apple cider
⅓ cup packed light brown sugar
½ tsp. ground ginger
½ tsp. cinnamon
¼ tsp. ground nutmeg
⅛ tsp. ground cloves
1 firm apple (such as Jazz or Sweet Tango), peeled, cored, and finely diced

1. Combine cranberries, orange zest, apple cider, brown sugar, ginger, cinnamon, nutmeg, cloves, and apple in a medium heavy saucepan over medium; cook, stirring, until sugar dissolves, about 2 minutes.

2. Reduce heat to low and simmer until cranberries soften and pop and sauce thickens, 20 to 25 minutes, stirring occasionally (sauce will thicken more as it chills).

3. Let cool, then cover and refrigerate until ready to serve.

Green Beans with Garlic Vinaigrette

SERVES **12**
ACTIVE **5 MIN.**
TOTAL **15 MIN.**

Toast the sliced almonds in a pie pan at 350°F for 5 to 10 minutes until fragrant and golden.

- ½ tsp. lemon zest
- 1 Tbsp. fresh lemon juice
- 2 tsp. extra-virgin olive oil
- 1 tsp. Dijon mustard
- ½ tsp. kosher salt
- ¼ tsp. black pepper
- 2 garlic cloves, minced
- 2½ lb. green beans, trimmed
- ⅓ cup sliced almonds, toasted
- 1 Tbsp. fresh thyme leaves

1. Whisk together lemon zest, lemon juice, olive oil, mustard, salt, pepper, and garlic in a small bowl. Set aside.

2. Bring large pot of generously salted water to a boil. Add the beans and cook until crisp-tender, 4 to 6 minutes. Drain.

3. Place beans in a large bowl. Add the lemon dressing; toss well to coat. Sprinkle with almonds and thyme.

Pro Tip:
HOW TO TRIM GREEN BEANS

The easiest way to trim green beans is to line them up on a cutting board and slice off the stem end that once connected the bean pod to the rest of the plant. You're probably familiar with snapping off the ends, but the slicing method is faster.

Only trim your beans when ready to cook, because the end can dry out if trimmed too far in advance. This is why you should avoid buying pretrimmed beans at the grocery store; you'll end up trimming the dried bits off anyhow. While you can flip the beans and trim the wispy ends as well, they are edible and can be quite pretty to keep in a dish.

Two-Potato Gratin

SERVES **8**
ACTIVE **15 MIN.**
TOTAL **1 HOUR, 15 MIN.**

Nutty Gruyère and fresh sage and thyme add so much flavor to this classic gratin. This can be baked ahead and reheated. Be sure to add the thyme garnish just before serving.

- **Nonstick cooking spray**
- **1 Tbsp. chopped fresh sage**
- **1 Tbsp. chopped fresh thyme**
- **2 lb. russet potatoes, peeled, sliced ⅛ inch thick**
- **2 lb. sweet potatoes, peeled, sliced ⅛ inch thick**
- **1½ tsp. kosher salt**
- **½ tsp. black pepper**
- **1½ cups half-and-half**
- **½ cup lower-sodium chicken broth**
- **1½ cups grated Gruyère cheese**
- **Fresh thyme leaves, for garnish (optional)**

1. Preheat oven to 425°F. Line a large, rimmed baking sheet with foil. Lightly spray a 3-quart shallow microwave- and oven-safe baking dish with cooking spray. Combine sage and chopped thyme in a small bowl.

2. Layer one-third of the russet potatoes and sweet potatoes in prepared dish, alternating the slices. Sprinkle with one-third of herb mixture and about one-third each of the salt and pepper. Repeat layering three times.

3. Combine half-and-half and broth in a large measuring cup and pour over potatoes. Place dish on baking sheet and cover with foil. Bake in preheated oven 50 minutes. Uncover, sprinkle with cheese, and bake until golden and bubbly, 20 to 25 minutes longer

4. Let stand 10 minutes before serving. Garnish with fresh thyme leaves, if desired.

Dry-Brined Turkey with Pecan Gremolata

SERVES **8 TO 10** • ACTIVE **20 MIN.** • TOTAL **3 HOURS, 25 MIN., PLUS 12 HOURS BRINING**

Aside from the aromatics placed in the cavity, this bird is seasoned only with salt and pepper—you will be shocked by how deeply flavorful it turns out. This recipe goes to show that sometimes simple really is best. The dry brine not only lends this turkey so much depth of flavor, but gives it extra-crisp skin.

- 1 (12- to 14-lb.) fresh (or thawed frozen) whole turkey, patted dry using paper towels, with giblets and neck removed
- 2 Tbsp. kosher salt
- 1 Tbsp. black pepper
- 1 medium yellow onion, unpeeled and quartered lengthwise
- 3 dried bay leaves
- 1 garlic head, halved crosswise
- 5 (5-inch) thyme sprigs, plus more for garnish
- 5 (6-inch) rosemary sprigs, plus more for garnish
- 2 Tbsp. olive oil
- Pecan Gremolata (recipe follows)

1. Line a large roasting pan with aluminum foil, and fit a roasting rack inside pan. Sprinkle turkey evenly with salt and pepper. Place turkey, breast side up, on prepared roasting rack. Chill, uncovered, at least 12 hours or up to 48 hours.

2. Remove turkey from refrigerator, and let stand at room temperature 20 to 30 minutes. Meanwhile, preheat oven to 450°F with rack in lower-third position.

3. Place onion quarters, bay leaves, garlic halves, thyme sprigs, and rosemary sprigs inside turkey cavity. Tie legs together with kitchen twine; tuck wing tips under. Lightly brush turkey with oil, being careful not to brush off the seasoning from skin.

4. Roast in preheated oven on lower-third rack until golden brown and crispy, about 45 minutes. Without removing from oven, carefully cover turkey loosely with foil; reduce oven temperature to 350°F. Roast until a thermometer inserted into thickest portion of thigh registers 165°F, 1 hour, 30 minutes to 2 hours, 30 minutes. Transfer turkey to a cutting board; let rest, loosely covered with foil, for 30 minutes.

5. Remove and discard mixture inside cavity. Carve turkey into about 1-inch slices. If desired, reserve pan drippings for making a gravy. Arrange carved turkey on a platter. Garnish with additional thyme and rosemary sprigs.

PECAN GREMOLATA

Stir together 1 cup finely chopped fresh flat-leaf parsley; ⅔ cup finely chopped toasted pecans; 2 Tbsp. lemon zest; 4 garlic cloves, minced; and ½ tsp. kosher salt in a small bowl. Makes about 2 cups.

MULLED CIDER-CRANBERRY RELISH

Vanilla Layer Cake with Fruit-and-Herb Wreath

SERVES **10** • ACTIVE **30 MIN.** • TOTAL **1 HOUR, 50 MIN.**

For a smooth finish, dip a knife or offset spatula in hot water; then wipe it dry before frosting the cake.

- 1 (15¼-oz.) pkg. yellow cake mix (such as Duncan Hines Classic Yellow Cake Mix)
- Vanilla Buttercream (recipe follows)
- Raspberries, cranberries, pomegranate arils, fresh mint, rosemary, bay leaves, and stevia leaves, for garnish

1. Preheat oven to 350°F. Prepare cake batter according to package directions. Divide batter among 3 greased and floured 6-inch round cake pans. Bake in preheated oven until a wooden pick inserted into center comes out clean, about 25 minutes. Cool cake layers in pans on a wire rack 10 minutes. Invert cake layers onto rack; cool completely, about 45 minutes.

2. Prepare Vanilla Buttercream.

3. Using a serrated knife, trim domed tops of cake layers to make them even. Spread buttercream between layers and on top and sides of cake. Arrange a ring of garnishes around base of cake to form a wreath. Place a cluster of garnishes on top of cake.

VANILLA BUTTERCREAM

- 1½ cups unsalted butter, softened
- 5 cups unsifted powdered sugar
- 1 tsp. vanilla extract
- ¼ cup heavy whipping cream

Beat butter in bowl of a heavy-duty stand mixer fitted with the paddle attachment on medium until creamy, 1 to 2 minutes. Reduce speed to low; gradually add powdered sugar, beating until smooth, about 2 minutes, stopping to scrape sides of bowl as needed. Beat in vanilla. Gradually add cream, beating on medium until fluffy and spreadable, about 30 seconds. Makes about 6 cups.

Whip Up Sweet Surprises

Baking and Christmas go hand in hand. Whether you stir together sweets with family or host an afternoon of baking with friends, these recipes are perfect for this season of giving.

menu

Fresh Strawberry Truffles
Chocolate-Peppermint Thumbprints
Maple-Gingerbread People
Red Velvet–White Chocolate Cookies
Snowflake Sugar Cookies
Cranberry Shortbread Bars
Cappuccino-Walnut Toffee

ENTERTAIN

Fresh Strawberry Truffles

MAKES **2 DOZEN** • ACTIVE **20 MIN.** • TOTAL **20 MIN., PLUS 1 HOUR, 30 MIN. CHILLING**

Mix it up! One batch of this recipe can be split in half to make two different flavors of truffles. See variations below.

- 1 cup fresh strawberries, hulled
- 2⅓ cups (14 oz.) white chocolate chips (from 2 [11-oz.] pkg.)
- 1 Tbsp. heavy whipping cream
- 1 tsp. lemon zest (from 1 lemon)
- ¼ tsp. kosher salt
- Red liquid food coloring (optional)
- 2 Tbsp. pink sanding sugar
- 2 Tbsp. white sanding sugar

1. Place strawberries in a food processor or blender; process until smooth, stopping to scrape down sides as needed, about 30 seconds. Pour through a fine-mesh strainer into a small bowl, pressing pulp with the back of a spoon to release all juices; discard pulp. Measure ¼ cup strawberry juice.

2. Combine white chocolate chips, cream, and ¼ cup strawberry juice in a medium heatproof bowl. Microwave on HIGH in 15-second intervals, stirring after each interval, until melted (mixture will be thick), about 45 to 60 seconds total. Stir in lemon zest and salt until well combined. Stir in food coloring, if desired. Cover with plastic wrap, and refrigerate until firm, about 1½ to 2 hours.

3. Stir together pink and white sanding sugars in a shallow dish. Scoop chilled white chocolate mixture into 24 portions using the large side of a melon baller or a small (about 1¼ inches in diameter) cookie scoop. Working with 1 portion at a time and using hands, roll each portion into a ball, and place in sugar mixture, tossing gently to coat fully. Place on a parchment paper-lined baking sheet. Serve immediately, or store in an airtight container in refrigerator for up to 1 week or in freezer for up to 2 months. Let chilled truffles stand at room temperature for 30 minutes before serving. Or (if frozen) thaw truffles in refrigerator overnight.

VARIATIONS

Tipsy Strawberry Truffles: Prepare recipe as directed through Step 2, substituting 1 Tbsp. brandy and ¼ tsp. vanilla extract for 1 tsp. zest. Proceed with Step 3 as directed, substituting ¼ cup finely chopped (using a food processor) freeze-dried strawberries (from 1 [0.8-oz.] pkg.) for sanding sugars.

Creamy Strawberry-Vanilla Bean Truffles: Prepare recipe as directed through Step 2, substituting 2 tsp. vanilla bean paste for 1 tsp. zest. Scoop and roll chilled white chocolate mixture into balls as directed in Step 3. Microwave 1 (11-oz.) pkg. white chocolate chips in a medium-size heatproof bowl on HIGH in 30-second intervals, stirring after each interval, until melted, about 1 minute total. Reserve 2 Tbsp. melted white chocolate in a bowl. Using a fork, dip truffles, 1 at a time, in remaining melted white chocolate until fully coated, allowing excess to drip off. Place truffles on a parchment paper-lined baking sheet. Stir red liquid food coloring into reserved 2 Tbsp. melted white chocolate until desired color is reached. Using a fork, drizzle pink chocolate mixture over the dipped truffles. (Or transfer pink chocolate mixture to a small zip-top plastic freezer bag, cut a small hole in corner of bag, and pipe over dipped truffles.) Let truffles stand at room temperature until chocolate sets, about 15 minutes.

Strawberry-Coconut Truffles: Prepare recipe as directed, substituting 1 tsp. coconut extract for zest in Step 2 and 1¼ cups finely chopped sweetened flaked coconut for sanding sugars in Step 3.

Chocolate-Peppermint Thumbprints

MAKES ABOUT 4 DOZEN
ACTIVE 40 MIN.
TOTAL 1 HOUR, 30 MIN.

The chocolate filling for these thumbprints is impossibly rich and incredibly easy to make in the microwave.

- 1 cup unsalted butter, softened
- ¾ cup powdered sugar
- ¼ cup packed light brown sugar
- 1 large egg yolk
- 1 tsp. vanilla extract
- 3 cups all-purpose flour
- ½ tsp. kosher salt
- ½ tsp. baking powder
- ¾ cup semisweet chocolate chips
- 3 Tbsp. heavy whipping cream
- 2 Tbsp. crushed hard red peppermint candies (about 6 candies)
- 2 Tbsp. crushed hard green peppermint candies (about 6 candies)

1. Preheat oven to 375°F with oven racks in the top third and bottom third of oven. Combine butter, powdered sugar, and brown sugar in a large bowl; beat with an electric mixer on medium until smooth, about 1 minute. Add egg yolk and vanilla, and beat on low just until incorporated. Whisk together flour, salt, and baking powder in a small bowl, and gradually add to butter mixture, beating on low just until incorporated after each addition.

2. Drop dough by tablespoonfuls 1 inch apart onto parchment paper-lined baking sheets. Press your thumb or the end of a wooden spoon into each ball, forming an indentation.

3. Bake in preheated oven until cookies are set and beginning to brown, about 12 minutes, switching pans top rack to bottom rack halfway through baking. Cool on pans on wire racks 5 minutes; remove cookies to wire racks, and cool completely, about 30 minutes.

4. Combine chocolate chips and cream in a microwave-safe bowl, and microwave on MEDIUM (50% power) until melted and smooth, about 1½ minutes, stirring every 30 seconds. Cool 5 minutes. Fill each indentation with about ½ teaspoon of the ganache. Sprinkle half the cookies evenly with crushed red peppermints and remaining half with crushed green peppermints. Let stand at least 15 minutes before serving.

Maple-Gingerbread People

MAKES ABOUT 2½ DOZEN
ACTIVE 30 MIN.
TOTAL 2 HOURS, 10 MIN.

Gingerbread cookies never tasted so good!

- ¼ cup pure maple syrup
- 1 large egg
- 1 large egg yolk
- 3½ cups all-purpose flour
- 1 cup packed light brown sugar
- ½ cup granulated sugar
- 1 Tbsp. ground ginger
- 1 Tbsp. orange zest
- 2 tsp. ground cinnamon
- 1 tsp. ground cloves
- ½ tsp. kosher salt
- ½ tsp. baking soda
- 1 cup cold salted butter, cut into ½-inch pieces
- Royal Icing (recipe follows)

1. Whisk syrup, egg, and egg yolk in a bowl. Combine flour, brown sugar, granulated sugar, ginger, orange zest, cinnamon, cloves, salt, and baking soda in a food processor; process until combined, 1 minute. Add butter; pulse until mixture resembles coarse sand, 5 to 6 times. Add syrup mixture; pulse until it just clumps, 5 to 6 times.

2. Turn mixture out onto a lightly floured work surface, and knead until mixture comes together, 5 to 6 times. Divide dough in half; shape each half into a 4-inch disk. Wrap each disk in plastic wrap, and chill 1 hour or up to 2 days.

3. Preheat oven to 350°F. Unwrap 1 dough disk, and roll to ¼-inch thickness on a lightly floured surface. Cut with a 5- x 3-inch cookie cutter, rerolling scraps once. Place 1 inch apart on parchment paper-lined baking sheets.

4. Bake in preheated oven until set, 12 minutes. Cool on pans 2 minutes; remove cookies to wire racks, and cool completely for 30 minutes. Repeat with remaining dough.

5. Snip a very small opening in tip of a tipless piping bag. Pipe icing on cookies and decorate as desired.

ROYAL ICING

Combine 1½ cups powdered sugar, 1 Tbsp. meringue powder, and 4 teaspoons water in a medium bowl; beat with an electric mixer on medium until well combined, 4 to 5 minutes. Add up to 2 teaspoons water, ¼ teaspoon at a time, beating until desired consistency is reached.

Red Velvet–White Chocolate Cookies

MAKES 45 COOKIES
ACTIVE 30 MIN.
TOTAL 4 HOURS, INCLUDING 2 HOURS CHILLING

To add a nice crunch, stir ½ cup chopped nuts into the batter with the chopped white chocolate.

- 3 (4-oz.) white chocolate baking bars
- 1½ cups granulated sugar
- 1 cup unsalted butter, softened
- 2 large eggs
- 1 tsp. vanilla extract
- 2⅓ cups all-purpose flour
- 3 Tbsp. unsweetened cocoa
- 1 tsp. baking powder
- ½ tsp. baking soda
- ½ tsp. kosher salt
- 2 tsp. red food coloring gel

1. Coarsely chop 2 of the white chocolate baking bars. Set aside; reserve for folding into cookie dough batter. Coarsely chop remaining white chocolate baking bar. Set aside; reserve for pressing into cookie dough balls. Beat sugar and butter with a stand mixer fitted with a paddle attachment on medium until light and fluffy, about 2 minutes. Add eggs and vanilla; beat just until combined, about 20 seconds, stopping to scrape down sides of bowl as needed.

2. Whisk together flour, cocoa, baking powder, baking soda, and salt in a medium bowl; add to butter mixture. Beat on low until smooth and combined, about 2 minutes. Add red food coloring; beat on medium until just incorporated, about 30 seconds. Fold the 2 reserved chopped baking bars into batter. Cover bowl, and chill at least 2 hours or up to overnight.

3. Preheat oven to 350°F. Line 3 baking sheets with parchment paper. Remove dough from refrigerator, and unwrap. Scoop 15 dough balls by heaping tablespoonfuls; shape into 1½-inch balls. Arrange 2 inches apart on one prepared baking sheet. (Return remaining dough in bowl to refrigerator until ready to bake.) Press about one-third of the reserved chopped baking bar into tops of dough balls. Bake in preheated oven until tops are crackled and edges are set, 9 to 10 minutes. Remove from oven; cool on baking sheet 15 minutes. Transfer cookies to a wire rack, and cool completely, about 30 minutes. Repeat procedure twice with remaining dough and chopped baking bar.

Snowflake Sugar Cookies

MAKES 2 DOZEN
ACTIVE 25 MIN.
TOTAL 1 HOUR, 15 MIN.

Every baker needs a classic sugar cookie in their repertoire. This is a keeper for your recipe box.

- 3 cups all-purpose flour
- 1 tsp. baking powder
- ¼ tsp. kosher salt
- 1 cup unsalted butter, softened
- 1 cup granulated sugar
- 2 eggs, at room temperature
- 1 tsp. vanilla extract
- 1 tsp. almond extract
- Royal Icing (page 84)
- White sanding sugar or edible glitter (optional)

1. Combine flour, baking powder, and salt; set aside.

2. Beat butter and sugar until smooth. Add eggs, vanilla extract, and almond extract; beat until combined. Gradually add flour mixture; beat on low until smooth. Divide dough in half and shape into disks. Wrap in plastic wrap and chill.

3. Preheat oven to 375°F. Roll 1 disk at a time on a lightly floured surface to ¼-inch thickness. Cut with a snowflake cookie cutter and space 2 inches apart on parchment paper–lined baking sheets. Refrigerate to help cookies keep their shape.

4. Bake in preheated oven 8 to 10 minutes, rotating halfway through baking. Cool on wire racks. Repeat process with remaining dough.

5. Make Royal Icing. Snip a very small opening (about ¼ inch) in tip of 1 tipless piping bag (for piping-consistency icing). Snip a slightly larger opening (about ½ inch) in tip of 1 tipless piping bag (for flooding-consistency icing).

6. Fill piping bag with half of the piping-consistency white Royal Icing. Mix an additional tablespoon of water (or amount needed to achieve flooding-consistency icing) into remaining Royal Icing. Fill flooding-consistency tipless piping bag with white flooding icing.

7. Outline snowflake cookies with white piping icing. Let dry for 1 to 2 minutes. Flood with white flooding icing. Let dry for 1 to 2 hours.

8. Using white piping-consistency icing, pipe desired pattern or design on snowflake cookies. Dip the iced cookies in sanding sugar or brush with edible glitter for shine.

Cranberry Shortbread Bars

MAKES **2 DOZEN**
ACTIVE **20 MIN.**
TOTAL **2 HOURS, 5 MIN.**

Freeze the shortbread dough, and then grate it in a food processor to get the most tender crust.

- **1½ cups fresh or frozen cranberries**
- **¼ cup water**
- **1 cup granulated sugar, divided**
- **¾ cup butter, softened, plus more for greasing pan**
- **¼ tsp. kosher salt**
- **2 large egg yolks**
- **1 tsp. vanilla extract**
- **1¾ cups all-purpose flour**

1. Bring cranberries, water, and ¼ cup of the sugar to a boil in a small saucepan over medium-high. Cook, stirring and smashing berries occasionally, until mixture thickens, 10 to 12 minutes. Remove from heat, and cool completely.

2. Beat butter, salt, and remaining ¾ cup sugar in a large bowl with an electric mixer on medium until light and fluffy, 3 to 5 minutes. Add egg yolks and vanilla; beat on low speed until combined. Add flour to butter mixture; beat on low speed until combined.

3. Turn dough out onto a lightly floured work surface; knead until dough comes together, 3 to 4 times. Shape into a 14-inch-long log. Cover with plastic wrap, and freeze at least 1 hour or overnight.

4. Preheat oven to 350°F. Line a 9-inch square baking pan with parchment paper, allowing paper to extend past edges of pan. Grease paper.

5. Remove plastic wrap from dough log; cut in half crosswise, and cut each piece in half lengthwise. Feed dough log quarters through the chute of a food processor fitted with a shredding blade. Press half of grated dough into the bottom of prepared pan. Spread cranberry mixture over dough, leaving a ½-inch border. Top with remaining half of grated dough, pressing to seal edges.

6. Bake in preheated oven until firm and golden brown, 33 to 35 minutes. Cool in pan. Lift cranberry shortbread from pan using parchment as handles; cut into rectangles.

Cappuccino-Walnut Toffee

MAKES **ABOUT 2 POUNDS**
ACTIVE **35 MIN.**
TOTAL **2 HOURS, 18 MIN.**

Rich and buttery, this eye-opening confection is irresistible.

- **2 cups chopped walnuts**
- **1¼ cups butter**
- **1 cup granulated sugar**
- **⅓ cup firmly packed light brown sugar**
- **1 Tbsp. dark unsulphured molasses**
- **2 tsp. instant espresso**
- **½ tsp. ground cinnamon**
- **¼ tsp. kosher salt**
- **1 cup milk chocolate morsels**
- **1 cup white chocolate morsels**

1. Preheat oven to 350°F. Butter a 15- x 10-inch jelly-roll pan.

2. Bake walnuts in preheated oven in a single layer in a shallow pan 8 to 10 minutes or until toasted and fragrant, stirring halfway through. Let cool 30 minutes.

3. Melt 1¼ cups butter in a 3½-quart heavy saucepan over medium; stir in granulated sugar, brown sugar, molasses, espresso, cinnamon, salt, and ⅓ cup water. Cook, stirring constantly, until a candy thermometer registers 290°F (soft crack stage), about 20 minutes. Remove pan from heat, and stir in walnuts. Quickly pour mixture into prepared pan, and spread into an even layer. Immediately sprinkle milk chocolate and white chocolate morsels over top; let stand 5 minutes. Swirl chocolate using an offset spatula. Cover and chill until firm (about 1 hour). Break toffee into pieces. Store in an airtight container in refrigerator up to 7 days. Serve cold or at room temperature.

Dish Up Good Luck

Fortify yourself for good things to come in the year ahead with a New Year's feast built around ingredients that have symbolized good luck in the South and cultures beyond.

menu

Prosperity Punch
Good-Fortune Fish Dip
Confetti Chow Chow
Clementine-and-Collard Salad with Pomegranate Seeds
Cornmeal-Chive Biscuits
Classic Hoppin' John
Pepper Jelly and Ginger Glazed Ham
Almond "Surprise" Cakes

ENTERTAIN

Good-Fortune Fish Dip

SERVES 12
ACTIVE 20 MIN.
TOTAL 20 MIN.

Fish are another lucky food in many cultures. Because they swim in schools and have scales reminiscent of gleaming coins, they are considered a symbol of wisdom and abundance. Serve this rich, smoky spread with crackers, baguette slices, and crudités. If you can't find smoked whitefish, substitute an equal amount of smoked salmon.

- 2 (8-oz.) smoked whitefish fillets, skin removed
- 2 celery stalks, diced (about ½ cup)
- ½ cup cream cheese, at room temperature
- ½ cup thinly sliced scallions (about 5 scallions)
- ¼ cup mayonnaise
- ¼ cup chopped fresh flat-leaf parsley
- ¼ cup chopped fresh dill, plus more for garnish
- ¼ cup chopped dill pickles (from 2 pickles)
- ¼ cup fresh lemon juice (from 2 lemons)
- 1 Tbsp. drained capers, chopped
- 1 Tbsp. extra-virgin olive oil
- ½ tsp. cayenne pepper
- ½ tsp. garlic powder
- ½ tsp. onion powder
- ½ tsp. kosher salt, plus more to taste
- ½ tsp. black pepper, plus more to taste
- Crackers and crudités, for serving

1. Flake smoked fish into ¾-inch chunks in a medium bowl.

2. Stir together celery, cream cheese, scallions, mayonnaise, parsley, dill, pickles, lemon juice, capers, olive oil, cayenne, garlic powder, onion powder, salt, and black pepper until smooth. Gently fold in smoked fish until incorporated, leaving some chunks intact and being careful not to overmix. Add more salt and black pepper to taste. Garnish with additional fresh dill. Serve with crackers and crudités.

Confetti Chow Chow

MAKES ABOUT 3 CUPS
ACTIVE 25 MIN.
TOTAL 4 HOURS, 5 MIN.

This classic Southern condiment brings bright acidity to dishes like pork barbecue, hoppin' john, or ham on a biscuit. Like collards, cabbage's green leaves represent green bills. Eating cabbage isn't just healthy, it might make you wealthy too.

- 3 cups chopped fresh cabbage
- ¾ cup chopped onion
- ¾ cup chopped green tomatoes
- ½ cup chopped green bell pepper
- ½ cup chopped red bell pepper
- 1 Tbsp. pickling salt
- ¾ cup granulated sugar
- ½ cup white vinegar
- ¼ cup water
- ¾ tsp. mustard seeds
- ¼ tsp. celery seeds
- ¼ tsp. ground turmeric
- ½ tsp. dried crushed red pepper
- 1 jalapeño pepper, seeded and finely chopped

1. Stir together cabbage, onion, green tomatoes, bell peppers, and pickling salt. Cover and chill 2 to 8 hours.

2. Transfer mixture to a Dutch oven. Stir in sugar, vinegar, water, mustard seeds, celery seeds, turmeric, and crushed red pepper. Bring to a boil over medium-high; reduce heat to medium, and simmer 3 minutes. Cool to room temperature (about 30 minutes).

3. Stir in jalapeño pepper. Cover and chill at least 1 hour or up to 8 hours before serving.

Clementine-and-Collard Salad with Pomegranate Seeds

SERVES **8** • ACTIVE **20 MIN.** • TOTAL **20 MIN.**

This hearty salad stars a trio of lucky ingredients:

Mandarins, or clementines, are a staple of the Chinese Lunar New Year believed to bring good fortune, longevity, and fertility. In other traditions, the citrus symbolizes generosity and is placed in stockings or shoes during the holidays to represent the gold Saint Nicholas is said to have tossed down chimneys for the poor. Indeed, the sunny fruit was a rare treat in Europe in the 19th century, so receiving one was a luxury to be savored.

Collard green leaves, abundant during Southern winters, have long been associated with green backs, or dollar bills, so eating them was believed to bring riches in the coming year.

In Greece, pomegranates are thrown against doors at the stroke of midnight on New Year's Eve. The more seeds that fall out, the more good fortune will bless the home's occupants.

---

4 clementines, divided
2 Tbsp. apple cider vinegar
4 tsp. Dijon mustard
2 tsp. sorghum syrup or honey
½ tsp. black pepper
1¼ tsp. kosher salt, divided
½ cup extra-virgin olive oil
2 lb. collard greens, stemmed and cut into thin strips
4 small shallots, sliced
1 cup chopped toasted pecans
6 oz. crumbled goat cheese
1 cup (8 oz.) pomegranate arils

1. Squeeze juice from 2 clementines into a small bowl. (You should have about 4 tablespoons juice.) Add apple cider vinegar, Dijon mustard, sorghum syrup (or honey), black pepper, and 1 teaspoon of the kosher salt. Slowly add extra-virgin olive oil, whisking to combine.

2. Place collard greens and sliced shallots in a large bowl. Add ¼ cup dressing, and gently massage into greens mixture with hands until greens are wilted and tender, 1 minute. Reserve remaining dressing.

3. Peel and slice remaining 2 clementines into rings, and set aside. Place the greens mixture on a serving platter; top with chopped toasted pecans, crumbled goat cheese, and sliced clementines. Drizzle reserved dressing over salad, and sprinkle with the remaining ¼ teaspoon kosher salt and pomegranate arils.

GOOD-FORTUNE FISH DIP

CORNMEAL-CHIVE BISCUITS

PEPPER JELLY AND GINGER GLAZED HAM

Cornmeal-Chive Biscuits

MAKES ABOUT 16 BISCUITS
ACTIVE 20 MIN.
TOTAL 45 MIN.

No New Year's feast is complete without cornbread. As the Southern adage goes, "Peas for pennies, greens for dollars, and cornbread for gold."

Be sure to press straight down with a biscuit cutter or glass for higher-rising biscuits. If you twist the cutter, you'll seal the edges of the dough and the biscuits won't bake up as tall.

- 2 cups self-rising soft-wheat flour
- ½ cup self-rising yellow cornmeal mix
- ½ cup cold butter
- ⅓ cup chopped fresh chives
- 1 cup whole buttermilk
- 2 Tbsp. butter, melted

1. Preheat oven to 425°F. Combine flour and cornmeal in a large bowl. Cut the cold butter into ½-inch-thick slices. Sprinkle butter slices over flour mixture, and toss. Cut butter into flour mixture with a pastry blender until crumbly. Cover and chill 10 minutes. Stir in chives. Add buttermilk, stirring just until dry ingredients are moistened.

2. Turn dough out onto a floured surface, and knead 3 or 4 times, gradually adding additional self-rising flour as needed. With floured hands, pat dough into a ¾-inch-thick rectangle (about 9 x 5 inches); dust top with flour. Fold dough over itself in 3 sections, starting with short end (as if folding a letter-size piece of paper). Repeat 2 more times, beginning with patting dough into a rectangle.

3. Pat dough to ½-inch thickness. Cut with a 2-inch round cutter, and place, side by side, on a parchment paper–lined or lightly greased jelly-roll pan. (Dough rounds should touch.)

4. Bake in preheated oven until lightly browned, 13 to 15 minutes. Remove from oven; brush with melted butter.

Classic Hoppin' John

SERVES 6
ACTIVE 25 MIN.
TOTAL 1 HOUR, 30 MIN.

Double this classic good-luck recipe, depending on your crowd. Like many symbolic New Year's foods, black-eyed peas are a nod to "pennies" and have long been eaten for the riches they will bring in the year to come.

- 6 thick-cut bacon slices, chopped
- 4 celery stalks, sliced (about 1½ cups)
- 1 medium yellow onion, chopped (about 1½ cups)
- 1 small green bell pepper, finely chopped (about 1 cup)
- 3 garlic cloves, chopped
- 1 tsp. chopped fresh thyme
- ½ tsp. black pepper
- ¼ tsp. cayenne pepper
- 1½ tsp. kosher salt, divided
- 8 cups lower-sodium chicken broth
- 4 cups fresh or frozen black-eyed peas
- 2 Tbsp. olive oil
- 1½ cups uncooked Carolina Gold rice
- Fresh scallions, sliced, for garnish

1. Cook bacon in a Dutch oven over medium-high, stirring, 10 to 12 minutes. Add celery, onion, bell pepper, garlic, thyme, black pepper, cayenne, and 1 teaspoon of the salt. Cook, stirring occasionally, about 8 minutes. Add broth and black-eyed peas, and bring to a boil. Reduce heat, and simmer until peas are tender, about 40 minutes. Drain pea mixture, reserving cooking liquid. Return pea mixture and 1 cup of the cooking liquid to Dutch oven. Cover to keep warm; set aside.

2. Heat oil in a medium saucepan over medium-high. Add rice, and cook, stirring often, until fragrant and lightly toasted, 3 to 4 minutes. Stir in 3 cups of the reserved cooking liquid and remaining ½ teaspoon salt. Bring to a boil, and reduce heat to medium-low; cover and cook until rice is tender, 15 to 18 minutes. Fluff rice with a fork, and gently stir into pea mixture in Dutch oven. Stir in remaining cooking liquid, ¼ cup at a time, until desired consistency is reached. Sprinkle with sliced fresh scallions.

Pepper Jelly and Ginger Glazed Ham

SERVES **12** • ACTIVE **15 MIN.** • TOTAL **5 HOURS**

Pork is a Southern staple and its spot on the New Year's table is no exception. Because pigs move forward as they forage for food, they symbolize moving ahead, while their rotund bodies represent abundance and needs fulfilled.

You can use any supermarket bone-in or semi-boneless smoked ham for this recipe, but choose one brined in natural juices.

- 1 (9-lb.) smoked, fully cooked bone-in half ham (see Note)
- 1 Tbsp. olive oil
- 1 tsp. ground black pepper
- 2 cups Riesling or other white wine
- 2 Tbsp. whole black peppercorns
- 1 Tbsp. whole cloves
- 1 Tbsp. fennel seeds
- 2 bay leaves
- 6 cups ginger ale
- ½ cup red pepper jelly
- 1 Tbsp. whole grain Dijon mustard

1. Preheat oven to 350°F. Make shallow cuts in fat of ham 1 inch apart in a diamond pattern. Rub olive oil and ground pepper over ham. Place ham on a rack in a 14- x 11-inch roasting pan. Pour wine into bottom of pan; stir in peppercorns, cloves, fennel seeds, and bay leaves. Add 4 cups water. Cover pan loosely with aluminum foil.

2. Bake, covered, in preheated oven on lower oven rack 2 hours.

3. Meanwhile, bring ginger ale to a boil in a deep-sided 12-inch skillet over medium-high, and boil until reduced to about ¾ cup, 25 to 30 minutes. Remove from heat, and stir in pepper jelly until smooth.

4. Uncover ham, and baste with ginger ale mixture. Bake, uncovered, until a meat thermometer registers 160°F and ham is caramelized, about 2½ more hours, basting every 30 minutes with ginger ale mixture. (Shield ham with foil to prevent excessive browning.) Remove from oven; transfer to a serving platter, reserving 2 cups pan drippings. Let stand 20 minutes before carving.

5. Pour reserved drippings through a fine wire-mesh strainer into a medium saucepan; skim fat. Bring drippings to a boil over high heat, and boil until liquid is reduced to ¾ cup, 12 to 15 minutes. Remove from heat; stir in mustard. Serve with ham.

Note: To prepare a 12- to 14-lb. fully cooked bone-in ham, increase olive oil to 2 Tbsp., ground black pepper to 2 tsp., red pepper jelly to 1 cup, and mustard to 1½ Tbsp. Prepare recipe as directed, cooking ginger ale mixture 20 to 25 minutes or until reduced to 1½ cups in Step 3, reserving 3 cups drippings in Step 4, and cooking reserved drippings until reduced to 1½ cups in Step 5. Serves 18 to 24.

ENTERTAIN

Almond "Surprise" Cakes

SERVES **15** • ACTIVE **45 MIN.** • TOTAL **2 HOURS, 10 MIN.**

Even nonbakers can make these festive cakes with hidden surprises for good luck thanks to the convenience of boxed cake mix. Be sure to let your guests know that there is a surprise hidden in every cake, so eating carefully with a fork is key.

- 1 (15¼-oz.) pkg. vanilla cake mix (such as Betty Crocker Super Moist Favorites Vanilla Cake Mix)
- 1 tsp. almond extract
- Finely grated zest of 1 orange
- Vanilla Buttercream (page 79) made with almond extract
- 15 silver coins (dollars, quarters, nickels, dimes), scrubbed
- Sliced almonds, toasted
- Pomegranate arils
- Powdered sugar, for dusting

1. Preheat oven to 350°F. Prepare cake batter according to package directions, stirring the 1 teaspoon almond extract into batter. Pour batter into a greased and floured 13- x 9-inch baking pan. Bake in preheated oven until a wooden pick inserted in center comes out clean, 28 to 33 minutes. Cool cake in pan on a wire rack 10 minutes. Invert cake onto rack; cool completely, about 45 minutes.

2. Prepare the Vanilla Buttercream, substituting almond extract for the vanilla extract.

3. Cut out 15 mini cakes from cooled cake using a 2½-inch round cutter. Slice each mini cake in half horizontally, making 2 layers per mini cake. Using a small offset spatula, spread Vanilla Buttercream on half of layers. Press a clean silver coin into the buttercream in the center of each cake. Top with remaining layers. Cover tops and sides of cakes with buttercream and decorate the cakes with almonds and pomegranate arils.

4. Right before serving, use a fine-mesh strainer to dust lightly with powdered sugar.

ENTERTAIN

SAVOR

holiday cookbook

Take a Dip

When it comes to party crowd-pleasers, these tasty dips are slam dunks.

recipes

Beer-Cheese Fondue
Preserved Lemon Labneh Dip
Classic Rémoulade with Boiled Shrimp
Warm Gumbo Dip
Gorgonzola Cheesecake with Pear Preserves and Pecans

Beer-Cheese Fondue

SERVES **8**
ACTIVE **15 MIN.**
TOTAL **15 MIN.**

Whether you're swapping gifts with girlfriends, hosting a family get-together, or having the whole block over after caroling, this festive fondue satisfies.

- ¼ cup unsalted butter
- ⅓ cup all-purpose flour
- 1 (12-oz.) bottle lager beer (such as Yuengling)
- ¼ cup heavy whipping cream
- 6 oz. Gruyère cheese, shredded (about 1½ cups)
- 6 oz. mild cheddar cheese, shredded (about 1½ cups)
- ½ tsp. Worcestershire sauce
- ½ tsp. dry mustard

Melt butter in a medium saucepan over medium-low. Gradually whisk in flour. Cook, whisking constantly, until lightly browned, about 1 minute. Gradually whisk in beer and cream. Cook, whisking constantly, until sauce has thickened and begins to bubble, about 3 minutes. Gradually add Gruyère and Cheddar, whisking constantly, allowing each addition to melt and become incorporated before adding more. Whisk in Worcestershire sauce and dry mustard until smooth. Transfer mixture to a fondue pot; cover and keep warm. Serve immediately.

Serving suggestions: Cubed bread, sliced cooked bratwurst, steamed broccoli florets, roasted halved Brussels sprouts, roasted halved fingerling potatoes.

Preserved Lemon Labneh Dip

MAKES **1 CUP**
ACTIVE **5 MIN.**
TOTAL **5 MIN.**

Labneh (LEB-neigh) is a strained yogurt with a rich texture similar to whipped cream cheese. It can be used as a bagel spread or drizzled with olive oil and sprinkled with spices for a tasty dip like this tangy, rich, salty, and citrusy one.

- 1 cup Homemade Labneh (recipe follows)
- ½ preserved lemon, finely chopped and seeds removed
- 1 tsp. black pepper
- 1 Tbsp. extra-virgin olive oil
- ½ tsp. ground sumac

Combine labneh and preserved lemon in a medium bowl; season with black pepper. Place mixture in a serving bowl. Drizzle with olive oil; sprinkle with ground sumac. Serve with flatbreads and vegetables.

HOMEMADE LABNEH

- 2 cups plain whole-milk yogurt (not Greek style)
- ½ tsp. kosher salt

1. Arrange a double layer of cheesecloth in a strainer (or, alternatively, line a strainer with coffee filters); spoon yogurt into strainer, and place strainer over a bowl so that it rests a few inches above the bottom of the bowl. Lightly cover strainer with plastic wrap. Refrigerate 24 hours.

2. Remove strainer from bowl; discard whey. Spoon labneh into a bowl; stir in salt. Store in refrigerator for up to 1 week. Makes about 1¾ cups.

Classic Rémoulade with Boiled Shrimp

SERVES 8 • ACTIVE 10 MIN. • TOTAL 2 HOURS, 15 MIN., INCLUDING CHILLING

This elegant French appetizer is a cinch to make. Buy cooked tail-on shrimp to save even more time. Any leftover sauce is delicious with burgers and fries or used to bind egg salad.

- 1 cup mayonnaise
- ¼ cup minced shallots
- ¼ cup finely chopped pickles
- 2 Tbsp. coarsely chopped capers
- 2 Tbsp. chopped fresh flat-leaf parsley
- 2 Tbsp. whole-grain mustard or Creole mustard
- 2 Tbsp. fresh lemon juice
- 1 Tbsp. sriracha
- Boiled Shrimp (recipe follows), chilled
- Saltine crackers, for serving

Combine mayonnaise, shallots, pickles, capers, parsley, mustard, lemon juice, and sriracha in a bowl; stir well to combine. Cover and chill at least 1 hour or overnight to let flavors come together. Serve with chilled Boiled Shrimp and saltine crackers.

BOILED SHRIMP

- 3 quarts water
- 2 cups dry white wine (such as Sauvignon Blanc)
- ¼ cup Old Bay Seasoning
- 6 thyme sprigs
- 4 lemons, halved
- 4 bay leaves
- 2 lb. large raw shrimp, tail-on

Combine water, wine, Old Bay, thyme, lemons, and bay leaves in a large saucepan over high; bring to a boil. Add shrimp to pan and cook 3 minutes. Drain well. Cool to room temperature. Spread shrimp in a single layer on a tray. Transfer to the refrigerator; chill 2 hours. Serve with Classic Rémoulade and saltine crackers.

Old Bay Your Way

The recipe for Old Bay Seasoning is a closely guarded secret, but to approximate its distinctive flavor and make just enough for the recipe here, combine 1 Tbsp. each celery salt, hot paprika, and smoked paprika with ½ tsp. each dry mustard, freshly ground black pepper, ground white pepper, and pumpkin pie spice. Mix in ¼ tsp. each ground bay leaves and cayenne. Makes about ¼ cup.

Warm Gumbo Dip

SERVES **8 TO 10** • ACTIVE **35 MIN.** • TOTAL **1 HOUR**

This dip boasts all the South Louisiana flavor of traditional gumbo without the need to make a roux. It easily can be made ahead and then baked just before serving. It is a filling addition to any holiday cocktail party spread.

- ¼ cup butter
- 6 scallions, sliced
- 2 celery stalks, diced
- 1 cup chopped assorted bell peppers
- 1½ lb. cooked smoked sausage, sliced
- 1 garlic clove, minced
- 1½ tsp. Creole seasoning
- 1 (8-oz.) pkg. cream cheese
- ¾ cup sliced pickled okra
- ½ cup plus 2 Tbsp. grated Parmesan cheese, divided
- 2 Tbsp. chopped fresh flat-leaf parsley
- Toasted French bread baguette slices, for serving

1. Preheat oven to 400°F. Melt butter in a Dutch oven over medium; add scallions, celery, and bell peppers. Cook, stirring occasionally, until peppers are tender, 6 to 8 minutes. Stir in sausage, garlic, and Creole seasoning; cook, stirring occasionally, 2 minutes. Reduce heat to low; add cream cheese, stirring until cheese is melted. Remove from heat, and stir in okra and ½ cup Parmesan cheese. Spoon mixture into a 2-quart baking dish, and sprinkle with remaining 2 tablespoons Parmesan cheese.

2. Bake in preheated oven until bubbly and lightly browned, 25 to 30 minutes. Sprinkle with parsley. Serve with toasted French bread.

Gorgonzola Cheesecake with Pear Preserves and Pecans

SERVES **12** • ACTIVE **15 MIN.** • TOTAL **9 HOURS, 55 MIN., INCLUDING CHILLING**

Serve this sweet-and-savory party spread on a cake stand for an elegant presentation.

- ½ cup pecan or walnut halves
- 2 (8-oz.) pkg. cream cheese, softened
- 1 (8-oz.) pkg. Gorgonzola crumbles
- ½ cup sour cream
- 2 Tbsp. chopped fresh chives
- 1 Tbsp. chopped fresh parsley
- 2 large eggs
- 2 Tbsp. all-purpose flour
- Nonstick cooking spray
- 1 (11.5-oz.) jar pear preserves
- Crackers, seedless red grapes, and assorted vegetables, for serving

1. Preheat oven to 350 F. Bake pecans in a single layer in a shallow pan until lightly toasted and fragrant, 8 to 10 minutes, stirring halfway through. Reduce oven temperature to 325 F.

2. Beat cream cheese, Gorgonzola, sour cream, chives, and parsley in a medium bowl with an electric mixer on medium until blended. Add eggs, 1 at a time, beating just until yellow disappears after each addition; fold in flour. Lightly grease a 7-inch springform pan with cooking spray. Spoon mixture into pan.

3. Bake until set, about 1 hour. Run a knife around outer edge of cheesecake to loosen from sides of pan. Let cool in pan on a wire rack 30 minutes. Cover and chill 8 hours.

4. Remove sides of pan. Transfer cheesecake to a platter, and spoon preserves over top; sprinkle with pecans. Serve with crackers, red grapes, and assorted vegetables.

Main Pleasers

Give these slow-cooked dishes a starring role on menus during this season of feasting.

recipes

Pumpernickel Roast Beef
Pork Roast with Apples, Bacon, and Cabbage
Coq au Vin
Monday Red Beans & Rice

Pumpernickel Roast Beef

SERVES **6** • ACTIVE **25 MIN.** • TOTAL **8 HOURS, 25 MIN.**

After a quick browning in a skillet to develop a richly flavored crust, a slow cooker gets this showstopping roast across the finish line, giving you time to check off things on your holiday hit list.

---

1 (4-lb.) sirloin tip roast

1 (10-oz.) pkg. frozen pearl onions

1 (12-oz.) bottle dark beer

¼ cup stone-ground mustard

1 Tbsp. caraway seeds

1½ tsp. kosher salt

1 tsp. black pepper

⅓ cup all-purpose flour

Hot buttered egg noodles, for serving

Fresh flat-leaf parsley leaves, for garnish

1. Brown the roast on all sides in a skillet over medium-high, about 10 minutes. Place onions in a 4-quart slow cooker; place browned roast on top. Add beer, mustard, caraway seeds, salt, and pepper.

2. Cook, covered, on LOW 8 hours or until roast is tender. Remove roast and onions, reserving drippings in cooker.

3. Turn cooker to HIGH. Whisk flour into reserved drippings; cook 10 minutes or until thickened. Serve with roast, onions, and buttered noodles. Garnish all with parsley leaves.

Pro Tip:
USING THE SLOW COOKER'S WARM SETTING

The WARM setting is not for cooking, but for keeping already-cooked foods at ideal serving temperature until you are ready to serve. To prevent food from dropping below food-safe temperatures, you shouldn't use the WARM setting for more than 4 hours.

Pork Roast with Apples, Bacon, and Cabbage

SERVES **6 TO 8** · ACTIVE **50 MIN.** · TOTAL **3 HOURS, 50 MIN.**

Apples give this festive roast a touch of sweetness to balance the salty, smoky savoriness of bacon and the tang of sauerkraut.

- 1 (3-lb.) boneless pork loin
- ½ tsp. kosher salt, plus more to taste
- ½ tsp. black pepper, plus more to taste
- 6 oz. thinly sliced pancetta or bacon
- Kitchen string
- 2 Tbsp. olive oil
- 2 small onions, quartered (root ends intact)
- 1 (12-oz.) pkg. frozen pearl onions (about 2 cups)
- 2 garlic cloves, thinly sliced
- 3 fresh thyme sprigs
- 2 bay leaves
- 1 (12-oz.) bottle stout or porter beer
- 2 Tbsp. Dijon mustard
- 3 firm apples (such as Gala), divided
- 2 cups jarred sauerkraut, rinsed
- 1½ cups finely shredded green cabbage
- ½ cup finely shredded purple cabbage
- 1 Tbsp. chopped fresh flat-leaf parsley
- 1 tsp. fresh lemon juice
- ½ cup apricot preserves
- ¼ cup chicken broth
- Fresh flat-leaf parsley leaves and bay leaves, for garnish (optional)

1. Trim fat and silver skin from pork. Sprinkle pork with salt and pepper. Wrap top and sides of pork with pancetta. Tie with kitchen string, securing at 1-inch intervals.

2. Cook pork in hot oil in a large skillet over medium, turning occasionally, 15 minutes or until deep golden brown. Remove from skillet, reserving drippings in skillet.

3. Place quartered onions, pearl onions, garlic, thyme, and bay leaves in a 6-quart slow cooker; top with pork.

4. Add beer to reserved drippings in skillet, and cook over medium until liquid is reduced by half, about 8 minutes, stirring to loosen browned bits from bottom of skillet. Stir in mustard, and pour over pork. Cover and cook on HIGH 2 hours.

5. Peel 2 apples; cut into large wedges. Add apple wedges, sauerkraut, and cabbage to slow cooker; cover and cook until a meat thermometer inserted into thickest portion of pork registers 150°F and apples are tender, 1 to 2 more hours.

6. Cut remaining unpeeled apple into thin strips, and toss with chopped parsley and lemon juice. Season with salt and pepper to taste.

7. Combine preserves and broth in a small saucepan; cook over medium, stirring often, until melted and smooth, 4 to 5 minutes.

8. Brush pork with apricot mixture. Cut into slices; serve with onion mixture, apple-parsley mixture, and additional Dijon mustard. Garnish with parsley leaves and additional bay leaves, if desired.

Coq au Vin

SERVES **6** • ACTIVE **1 HOUR, 20 MIN.** • TOTAL **3 HOURS, 20 MIN.**

This variation on the classic French wine-braised chicken uses white instead of red wine, maintaining the cooked chicken's lovely golden hue.

---

6 chicken leg quarters (4 to 5 lb.)
Kosher salt
Black pepper
2 Tbsp. olive oil
12 (1-oz.) bacon slices, cut into ½-inch pieces
2 (8-oz.) pkg. fresh cremini mushrooms, chopped
2 celery stalks, chopped
1 medium yellow onion, chopped
2 garlic cloves, chopped
1 (6-oz.) can tomato paste
3 cups dry white wine
1 (32-oz.) container lower-sodium chicken broth
6 fresh thyme sprigs
2 fresh rosemary sprigs
1 (6-oz.) pkg. baby carrots
1 Tbsp. butter

1. Preheat oven to 350°F. Season chicken with salt and pepper to taste. Cook 3 chicken leg quarters in 1 Tbsp. hot oil in a large Dutch oven over medium-high until browned, about 5 minutes on each side. Remove and wipe Dutch oven clean. Repeat with remaining oil and chicken leg quarters.

2. Cook bacon in Dutch oven over medium until crisp, about 4 minutes on each side. Remove bacon, and drain on paper towels, reserving 2 tablespoons drippings in Dutch oven. Cook mushrooms, celery, and onion in drippings over medium-high until browned, about 6 minutes. Stir in garlic; cook 1 minute. Stir in tomato paste and 1 cup wine; cook over medium-high, stirring often, 2 minutes. Add remaining 2 cups wine, and bring mixture to a boil. Boil, stirring occasionally, until reduced by half, about 5 minutes.

3. Add chicken and bacon to mushroom mixture in Dutch oven. Add broth, thyme, rosemary, and carrots; bring mixture to a simmer. Place a piece of parchment paper directly on chicken mixture, and cover Dutch oven with a tight-fitting lid.

4. Bake in preheated oven until meat pulls away from the bone, about 1½ hours. Let chicken stand in Dutch oven, covered with parchment and lid, at room temperature 30 minutes. Discard parchment paper.

5. Preheat broiler with oven rack 7 inches from heat. Remove chicken from Dutch oven, reserving vegetables and cooking liquid in Dutch oven. Place chicken on a lightly greased wire rack in a broiler pan.

6. Broil chicken until skin is crisp and golden brown, about 2 minutes. Transfer chicken to a serving platter; cover with aluminum foil. Skim fat from cooking liquid. Discard herb sprigs. Bring cooking liquid to a simmer over medium-high, stirring occasionally. Remove from heat. Add butter, and whisk until butter is melted and sauce is smooth. Serve sauce with chicken.

Pro Tip:
CHOOSING THE RIGHT PAN FOR THE JOB

A Dutch oven made of cast iron—or enameled cast iron—with a tight-fitting lid is the best for slow cooking. Cast iron is heavy and a good, even conductor of heat. Thin aluminum, other metal, or clay pots can have hot spots and burn food easily, leaving a bitter, scorched flavor that will permeate the dish.

Monday Red Beans & Rice

SERVES 10 TO 12 • ACTIVE 30 MIN. • TOTAL 3 HOURS, 55 MIN.

Tradition is big in New Orleans, and enjoying a big pot of red beans and rice on Monday is no exception. French-speaking Haitians brought the humble dish to the Crescent City in the 1700s. Cooks utilized the bones from Sunday's supper in a Monday stew that could slowly simmer on the stove all day while the week's chores were tackled. The result was a flavorful pot of smoky goodness delicious enough to be served any day.

- 1 (16-oz.) pkg. dried red kidney beans
- 1 lb. mild smoked sausage, cut into ¼-inch-thick slices
- 1 (½-lb.) smoked ham hock, cut in half
- ¼ cup vegetable oil
- 3 celery stalks, diced
- 1 medium yellow onion, diced
- 1 green bell pepper, diced
- 3 bay leaves
- 3 garlic cloves, chopped
- 2 Tbsp. salt-free Cajun seasoning
- 1 tsp. kosher salt
- 1 tsp. dried thyme
- 1 tsp. black pepper
- 3 (32-oz.) containers lower-sodium chicken broth
- Hot cooked rice, for serving

1. Place beans in a large Dutch oven; add water 2 inches above beans. Boil 1 minute; cover, remove from heat, and let stand 1 hour. Drain.

2. Cook sausage and ham in hot oil in Dutch oven over medium-high until browned, 8 to 10 minutes. Drain sausage and ham on paper towels, reserving 2 tablespoons drippings. Add celery, onion, bell pepper, bay leaves, garlic, Cajun seasoning, salt, thyme, and black pepper to drippings; cook over low heat, stirring occasionally, 15 minutes.

3. Add broth, beans, sausage, and ham to Dutch oven. Bring to a simmer. Cook, stirring occasionally, until beans are tender, about 2 hours. Discard ham hock and bay leaves. Serve with hot cooked rice.

What Is a Ham Hock?

Smoky, salty, and collagen-rich, the ham hock, or pork knuckle, is the joint that connects the pig's leg to the foot. Hocks are typically cured with salt and smoked, imparting a bacony flavor to simmered dishes. You can substitute a ham bone, smoked bacon, or smoked sausage in a pinch. If you are going pork-free, try smoked turkey sausage or turkey bacon. To keep a dish vegetarian, smoked paprika and an extra sprinkle of salt can capture some of the qualities of ham hock.

Bring In the Greens

Round out your Southern holiday dinners with these vibrant, comforting side dishes.

recipes

Asparagus with Cheese Sauce and Breadcrumbs
Brussels Sprouts with Maple Syrup and Pecans
Floret Medley with Cheese Straw Crumbs
Creamed Greens with Garlic Crust

Asparagus with Cheese Sauce and Breadcrumbs

SERVES 8 • ACTIVE 25 MIN. • TOTAL 25 MIN.

Blanketed with cheesy sauce and topped with lemony breadcrumbs, roasted asparagus becomes pure holiday comfort food.

- **2 Tbsp. unsalted butter**
- **½ cup panko breadcrumbs**
- **½ tsp. crushed red pepper**
- **¼ tsp. plus ⅛ tsp. kosher salt, divided**
- **3 Tbsp. finely chopped fresh flat-leaf parsley**
- **1 Tbsp. finely chopped fresh tarragon**
- **2 lb. medium fresh asparagus spears, trimmed**
- **1 Tbsp. olive oil**
- **½ cup heavy whipping cream**
- **4 oz. Parmigiano-Reggiano cheese, finely shredded (about 1½ cups)**
- **1 tsp. lemon zest (from 1 small lemon)**

1. Melt butter in a small skillet over medium-high. Add panko, crushed red pepper, and ⅛ teaspoon of the salt. Cook, stirring often, until toasted, 2 to 3 minutes. Stir in parsley and tarragon; set aside.

2. Preheat broiler to high with rack in middle position. Place asparagus on a rimmed baking sheet, and drizzle with olive oil; toss to coat. Sprinkle with remaining ¼ teaspoon of the salt, and broil until asparagus is tender-crisp, about 5 minutes (do not stir).

3. While asparagus broils, place cream in a small skillet. Bring to a gentle simmer over medium, stirring occasionally. Add Parmigiano-Reggiano ¼ cup at a time, stirring until completely melted and smooth after each addition.

4. Arrange broiled asparagus on a platter. Spoon cheese sauce over asparagus, and sprinkle with panko mixture and lemon zest.

Brussels Sprouts with Maple Syrup and Pecans

SERVES **4** • ACTIVE **30 MIN.** • TOTAL **30 MIN.**

The bitterness of Brussels sprouts is tempered by maple syrup's sweetness, while a splash of vinegar adds a bright note. If you wish, substitute honey or molasses for the maple syrup.

- 2 Tbsp. vegetable oil
- 1 lb. Brussels sprouts, halved lengthwise (about 4⅓ cups)
- 1 tsp. kosher salt
- Black pepper to taste, plus more for garnish
- 1 Tbsp. finely chopped shallot
- 2 Tbsp. pure maple syrup
- 1½ tsp. red wine vinegar
- 3 Tbsp. toasted pecan pieces
- 1 Tbsp. chopped fresh flat-leaf parsley
- 1 Tbsp. chopped fresh cilantro

1. Pour oil into a cold 12-inch cast-iron skillet. Working in batches, arrange Brussels sprouts, cut side down, in a single layer in skillet. Place skillet over medium-high, and cook, undisturbed, until cut sides of sprouts are very caramelized and sprouts are tender-crisp, 6 to 10 minutes. Transfer to a bowl or platter; stir in salt until well combined, and season with pepper to taste.

2. Whisk together shallot, maple syrup, and vinegar in a small bowl until well combined. Drizzle mixture over warm Brussels sprouts. Sprinkle with pecans, parsley, cilantro, and additional pepper.

Pro Tip:
STORING BRUSSELS SPROUTS

Remove damaged or loose outer leaves and trim the ends of fresh Brussels sprouts. Store the unwashed Brussels sprouts in a zip-top or produce bag in the refrigerator's crisper drawer for up to a couple of weeks. Rinse them just before use. If you find Brussels sprouts on the stalk, buy them! Sprouts on the stalk stay fresher longer than loose sprouts. Store the stalks in water, like flowers in a vase, in the refrigerator and cut them from the stalk when ready to use.

Floret Medley with Cheese Straw Crumbs

SERVES 6 • ACTIVE 20 MIN. • TOTAL 20 MIN.

Cheese straws are the delicious secret to this colorful vegetable medley's crunchy topping. Use your favorite brand or homemade cheese straws. Parmesan crisps are a worthy substitute.

- **1½ lb. (2-inch) mixed broccoli and multicolor cauliflower florets**
- **¼ cup olive oil**
- **1½ tsp. kosher salt**
- **½ tsp. black pepper**
- **Cheese Straw Crumbs (recipe follows)**

1. Place an aluminum foil-lined baking sheet on middle rack in oven; preheat oven to 425°F.

2. Place broccoli in a large bowl; toss with olive oil, salt, and pepper until fully coated. Once oven has preheated, carefully spread vegetables evenly over hot baking sheet, using a rubber spatula and scraping remaining olive oil and seasonings from bowl over vegetables. Roast until browned and crisp-tender, 14 to 16 minutes, tossing halfway through. Transfer to a serving platter. Sprinkle with Cheese Straw Crumbs, and serve.

CHEESE STRAW CRUMBS

Melt 2 Tbsp. butter in a large skillet over medium-high. Crumble 1½ cups cheese straws into skillet, and cook, stirring occasionally, until toasted, 2 to 3 minutes. Remove from heat, and stir in 1 tsp. fresh thyme leaves. Makes about 1 cup.

Creamed Greens with Garlic Crust

SERVES **6** • ACTIVE **30 MIN.** • TOTAL **45 MIN.**

Kale and mustard greens cook up tender in this creamy, crusty casserole, guaranteed get anyone to eat their vegetables.

Nonstick cooking spray

2 cups fresh breadcrumbs

¼ cup olive oil, divided

3 large garlic cloves, finely chopped, divided

1¼ tsp. kosher salt, divided

½ cup chopped yellow onion (from 1 small onion)

3 (8-oz.) bunches fresh Lacinato kale, stemmed and thinly sliced (about 10 cups)

1 (1-lb.) bunch fresh mustard greens, stemmed and thinly sliced (about 8 cups)

6 oz. cream cheese

4 oz. Fontina cheese, shredded (about 1 cup)

1 cup half-and-half

¼ tsp. black pepper

¼ tsp. crushed red pepper (optional)

1. Preheat oven to 450°F. Lightly coat a 2-quart baking dish with cooking spray. Stir together breadcrumbs, 2 tablespoons of the oil, one-third of the garlic, and ¼ teaspoon of the salt in a medium bowl; set aside.

2. Heat remaining 2 tablespoons oil in a Dutch oven over medium-high. Add onion, and cook, stirring often, until softened, about 5 minutes. Add remaining garlic, and cook 30 seconds. Add kale, mustard greens, and 3 tablespoons water. Cook, stirring often, until greens are wilted and tender, 10 to 12 minutes. Add cream cheese, Fontina, half-and-half, black pepper, remaining 1 teaspoon salt, and, if desired, crushed red pepper. Cook, stirring constantly, until just heated through, about 8 minutes.

3. Transfer to prepared baking dish, and sprinkle with breadcrumb mixture. Bake in preheated oven until golden and bubbly, about 15 minutes.

Party Dressing

Leave the stuffing to sofas and teddy bears.
In the South, dressing is fit for the birds
and so much more.

recipes

Brown Butter Cornbread Dressing
Cornbread Dressing with Green Chile and Chorizo
Fennel-and-Fruit Wild Rice Dressing
Savory Mushroom and Herb Dressing

Brown Butter Cornbread Dressing

SERVES **10 TO 12** • ACTIVE **15 MIN.** • TOTAL **1 HOUR, 45 MIN.**

Brown butter adds rich nuttiness to this versatile classic that is a welcome addition to any holiday feast.

Nonstick cooking spray

1 Tbsp. canola oil

1 medium yellow onion, chopped (about 1½ cups)

2 garlic cloves, minced

1 Tbsp. chopped fresh thyme, plus more for garnish

Brown Butter Cornbread (recipe follows), cut into ½-inch cubes

4 cups lower-sodium chicken broth

4 large eggs, beaten

1 tsp. kosher salt

½ tsp. black pepper

1. Preheat oven to 350°F. Lightly coat a 13- x 9-inch baking dish with cooking spray.

2. Heat oil in a large skillet over medium-high. Add onion. Cook, stirring occasionally, until tender, 5 minutes. Add garlic and thyme. Cook, stirring constantly, until fragrant, 1 minute. Remove from heat.

3. Stir together cornbread cubes, broth, eggs, salt, pepper, and onion mixture in a large bowl until well combined. Spoon cornbread mixture into prepared dish; let stand 30 minutes at room temperature to allow liquid to absorb into dry ingredients. Cover with aluminum foil.

4. Bake in preheated oven for 45 minutes. Uncover; continue baking until golden brown and set, about 15 minutes. Garnish with additional thyme.

BROWN BUTTER CORNBREAD

SERVES **8** • ACTIVE **15 MIN.** • TOTAL **50 MIN.**

½ cup unsalted butter

2 cups plain yellow cornmeal

1 cup all-purpose flour

1 Tbsp. baking powder

1½ tsp. kosher salt

1 tsp. granulated sugar

2½ cups whole buttermilk

1 large egg

1. Preheat oven to 425°F. Place butter in a 10-inch cast-iron skillet, and place in oven until butter is browned, about 8 minutes.

2. Meanwhile, whisk together cornmeal, flour, baking powder, kosher salt, and granulated sugar in a large bowl. Remove skillet from oven. Carefully pour 6 tablespoons of the melted brown butter into a small heatproof bowl; reserve remaining brown butter in skillet.

3. Whisk together buttermilk, egg, and the 6 tablespoons brown butter in a separate large bowl. Make a well in center of cornmeal mixture, and add buttermilk mixture, stirring until just combined. Pour batter into remaining brown butter in hot skillet.

4. Bake in preheated oven until cornbread is golden brown and a wooden pick inserted in center comes out clean, 25 to 28 minutes. Let cool completely, 35 to 40 minutes. Cut into ½-inch cubes to equal 12 cups if making Brown Butter Cornbread Dressing.

Cornbread Dressing with Green Chile and Chorizo

SERVES **6 TO 8** • ACTIVE **45 MIN.** • TOTAL **1 HOUR, 20 MIN.**

Chiles and chorizo add bold flavor and spice to the classic cornbread dressing.

Nonstick cooking spray

4 bacon slices, chopped

1 lb. fresh Mexican chorizo, casings removed

4 celery stalks, chopped

1 large sweet onion, chopped

2 (10-oz.) cans diced tomatoes with green chiles, drained

2 garlic cloves, minced

5 cups ½-inch cornbread cubes, toasted

2 cups cubed French bread

2 cups unsalted chicken broth

½ cup chopped fresh cilantro

½ cup butter, melted

2 Tbsp. chopped fresh oregano

2 large eggs, lightly beaten

Kosher salt

Black pepper

1. Preheat oven to 350°F. Lightly coat a 13- x 9-inch baking dish with cooking spray. Cook bacon in a skillet over medium until crisp, about 10 minutes, stirring occasionally. Remove bacon to a paper towel-lined plate to drain. Reserve drippings in skillet.

2. Cook chorizo in hot drippings, stirring often, until no longer pink, about 6 minutes. Place sausage and bacon in a large bowl. Cook celery, onion, and green chiles in hot drippings 10 minutes. Add garlic; cook 2 minutes. Stir celery mixture into sausage mixture.

3. Gently stir cornbread, French bread, broth, cilantro, butter, oregano, and eggs into sausage mixture. Season with salt and black pepper to taste. Spoon into prepared baking dish. Bake in preheated oven until golden, about 35 minutes.

Fennel-and-Fruit Wild Rice Dressing

SERVES **10** • ACTIVE **15 MIN.** • TOTAL **40 MIN.**

Wild rice, apples, fennel, and walnuts lend flavor and crunch to this colorful dressing.

- 5 sourdough or white bread slices, cut into ½-inch cubes (about 3 cups)
- 2 Tbsp. unsalted butter, melted
- 2 Tbsp. extra-virgin olive oil
- 2 medium celery stalks, chopped
- 1 small fennel bulb, chopped
- 1 medium red onion, diced
- 2 Honeycrisp or Fuji apples, diced
- 4 cups cooked wild rice
- 1 cup toasted walnuts, roughly chopped
- 2 Tbsp. chopped fresh flat-leaf parsley
- 1 Tbsp. chopped fresh sage
- 1 Tbsp. fresh lemon juice
- 2 tsp. kosher salt
- ½ tsp. black pepper
- ¼ cup firmly packed fresh flat-leaf parsley leaves

1. Preheat oven to 400°F. Toss bread cubes with melted butter in a medium bowl. Spread on a baking sheet, and bake in preheated oven until crispy and lightly browned, 5 to 8 minutes.

2. Heat oil in a skillet over medium-high. Add celery, fennel, and onion; cook, stirring occasionally, until tender, about 8 minutes. Add apples; cook, stirring occasionally, until apples are tender-crisp and browned, 5 to 7 minutes. Stir in toasted bread cubes, rice, walnuts, chopped parsley, chopped sage, lemon juice, salt, and pepper. Cook until heated through, about 3 minutes. Spoon onto a serving platter. Top with parsley leaves.

Savory Mushroom and Herb Dressing

SERVES **10** • ACTIVE **30 MIN.** • TOTAL **2 HOURS, 5 MIN.**

Eliminate the sausage and swap in vegetable broth for a vegetarian dressing.

- **6 Tbsp. unsalted butter, plus more for dish**
- **14 slices potato sandwich bread**
- **5 Tbsp. extra-virgin olive oil, divided**
- **10 oz. sweet Italian sausage, casings removed**
- **1 large yellow onion, coarsely chopped**
- **4 cups coarsely chopped celery, plus inner leaves for serving**
- **1 lb. portobello mushroom caps (about 4), halved and cut crosswise into ½-inch-thick slices**
- **Kosher salt and black pepper**
- **2 Tbsp. chopped fresh sage**
- **2 tsp. fresh thyme leaves**
- **½ cup chopped fresh flat-leaf parsley**
- **1½ cups unsalted chicken broth, divided**
- **2 large eggs**

1. Preheat oven to 350°F. Grease a 2½ to 3-quart baking dish or 9- x 13-inch casserole dish with butter. Bake bread on a rimmed baking sheet, turning once, until toasted, about 15 minutes. Cut into 1¼-inch pieces. Transfer to a large bowl.

2. Heat 1 tablespoon of the oil in a large skillet over medium-high. Add sausage and cook, breaking into bite-size pieces, until browned in places but not cooked through, 4 to 5 minutes. Transfer to bowl with bread.

3. Heat butter and remaining ¼ cup oil in skillet over medium. When butter melts and foam subsides, add onion, celery and mushrooms; season generously with salt and pepper. Cook, stirring occasionally, until vegetables are tender but no color has developed, 10 to 12 minutes. Transfer to bowl with bread mixture along with sage, thyme, parsley, and 1 cup of the broth; season with salt and pepper and gently toss to combine. Whisk eggs with remaining ½ cup broth. Pour over bread mixture and gently stir to combine. Transfer to prepared dish. Cover with buttered parchment, then foil.

4. Bake in preheated oven for 35 minutes. Uncover. Bake until top is crisp and golden, 35 to 45 minutes more. Let cool 10 minutes. Top with additional parsley and celery leaves.

Frosty Favorites

Surprise your guests with showstopping wintry wonders you can make weeks in advance.

recipes

Eggnog Baked Alaska
Cherries-and-Cream Icebox Cake
Turtle Sundaes
Frozen Café Mocha Tart

Eggnog Baked Alaska

SERVES **8 TO 10** • ACTIVE **1 HOUR** • TOTAL **14 HOURS, 35 MIN., INCLUDING CHILLING**

Get ready to wow your crowd! Cake mix cake and store-bought ice cream are anything but humble when topped with billows of caramelized meringue.

CAKE
Nonstick cooking spray
1 (15¼-oz.) pkg. red velvet cake mix (plus ingredients listed on box for preparing cake)

ICE CREAM
Nonstick cooking spray
½ gallon eggnog ice cream or vanilla ice cream, softened
1 Tbsp. freshly grated nutmeg
2 Tbsp. bourbon

SWISS MERINGUE
8 large egg whites
2 cups granulated sugar
1½ tsp. vanilla extract

1. Preheat oven to 350°F. Spray a 9-inch square cake pan with baking spray. Line with parchment paper. Coat parchment paper with baking spray.

2. Prepare Cake: Make cake mix according to package directions. Pour batter into prepared cake pan. Bake in preheated oven until a wooden pick inserted in center of cake comes out clean, 20 to 25 minutes. Cool in pan, about 10 minutes. Invert cake onto a wire rack; cool completely, about 45 minutes.

3. Prepare Ice Cream: Lightly coat a 9- x 4-inch Pullman pan (or 9- x 5-inch loaf pan) with cooking spray. Line pan with plastic wrap, allowing 4 to 5 inches to extend over sides.

4. Stir together softened ice cream, nutmeg, and bourbon. Spoon ice cream to within 1 inch of pan top. Cut cake in half vertically. Place one half on ice cream in pan. Cover and freeze several hours or up to 1 month.

5. Prepare Swiss Meringue: Pour water to a depth of 1½ inches into a small saucepan; bring to a boil over medium-high heat. Reduce heat to medium-low, and maintain at a simmer. Whisk together egg whites and granulated sugar in bowl of a heavy-duty electric stand mixer. Place bowl over simmering water, and cook, whisking constantly, 3 minutes or until sugar dissolves and a candy thermometer registers 140°F. Whisk in vanilla. Beat mixture at medium-high speed with stand mixer, using whisk attachment, until stiff peaks form and meringue has cooled completely, 8 to 10 minutes.

6. Remove cake and ice cream from freezer. Invert and unmold the cake onto a chilled serving plate. Remove plastic wrap. Spread meringue over top and sides, completely covering cake and ice cream. Brown meringue using a kitchen torch, holding torch 2 inches from meringue and moving torch back and forth. Serve immediately.

Cherries-and-Cream Icebox Cake

SERVES 12 • ACTIVE 25 MIN. • TOTAL 25 MIN., PLUS 8 HOURS CHILLING

Ribbons of pureed cherry preserves run through the layers of this dessert. Dollop a tablespoon of preserves into the center of each whipped cream layer. Use a wooden skewer or knife tip to drag and swirl the preserves outward and evenly throughout the whipped cream.

½ cup plus 1 Tbsp. cherry preserves (from 1 [13-oz.] jar, such as Bonne Maman)

4 cups heavy whipping cream, divided

2 tsp. vanilla extract, divided

¾ tsp. almond extract, divided

1 (8-oz.) pkg. cream cheese, softened

¾ cup plus 3 Tbsp. powdered sugar, divided

Nonstick cooking spray

21 (2¼- x 5-inch) graham crackers (from 1 [14.4-oz.] pkg.)

Fresh cherries, for topping

1. Process cherry preserves in a food processor until completely smooth, 1 to 2 minutes; set aside.

2. Beat 3 cups of the cream, 1 teaspoon of the vanilla, and ½ teaspoon of the almond extract in the bowl of a stand mixer fitted with the whisk attachment on medium until foamy, about 30 seconds. Increase speed to medium-high, and beat until stiff peaks form, 1 to 2 minutes; set aside.

3. Beat cream cheese, ¾ cup of the powdered sugar, and 3 tablespoons of pureed cherry preserves in a large bowl with an electric mixer on medium speed until smooth and completely combined, about 2 minutes. Gently fold one-third of whipped cream mixture into cream cheese mixture until thoroughly combined. Repeat in 2 more additions with remaining whipped cream mixture.

4. Lightly coat a 9-inch springform pan with cooking spray. Line bottom of pan with a layer of graham crackers, breaking them in order to cover bottom. (Don't worry about any small gaps.) Spread 2 cups whipped cream mixture over graham crackers. Dollop with 1 tablespoon pureed cherry preserves; swirl with a wooden skewer or the tip of a knife. Repeat layers 3 more times with remaining graham crackers and whipped cream mixture and 3 tablespoons of the remaining preserves, ending with whipped cream mixture and preserves. Cover; chill 8 to 24 hours.

5. Before serving, beat remaining 1 cup cream, 1 teaspoon vanilla, and ¼ teaspoon almond extract with a stand mixer fitted with whisk attachment on medium until foamy, about 30 seconds. Increase speed to medium-high, and gradually add remaining 3 tablespoons powdered sugar; beat until medium peaks form, 1 to 2 minutes. Remove cake from springform pan; spread top with whipped cream. Dollop remaining 1 tablespoon preserves onto whipped cream; swirl gently with a wooden skewer or the tip of a knife. Top with fresh cherries.

Turtle Sundaes

SERVES 12 • ACTIVE 15 MIN. • TOTAL 15 MIN., INCLUDING SAUCE

Turn store-bought ice cream into a stellar sweet ending with a simple homemade fudge drizzle, toasted nuts, and billows of whipped cream.

- **½ gallon salted-caramel ice cream**
- **Hot Fudge (recipe follows)**
- **1 cup toasted chopped pecans**
- **3 cups whipped cream (from 1½ cups heavy whipping cream)**

Place scoops of salted-caramel ice cream in short glasses. Drizzle each with a generous tablespoon of Hot Fudge. Top with toasted chopped pecans and a generous dollop of whipped cream.

HOT FUDGE

Cook ½ cup heavy whipping cream, ¼ cup butter, and ½ tsp. vanilla extract in a medium saucepan over medium-high, whisking often, until butter is melted. Whisk in ⅓ cup Dutch-process cocoa and ¼ cup each granulated sugar and dark brown sugar; cook, whisking often, until mixture thickens slightly, 2 to 3 minutes. Serve immediately. Let leftover Hot Fudge cool 20 minutes. Store in an airtight container in refrigerator for up to 2 weeks. To reheat, microwave on HIGH in 30-second intervals, stirring between intervals. Makes about 1 cup.

Frozen Café Mocha Tart

SERVES **10 TO 12** • ACTIVE **40 MIN.** • TOTAL **2 HOURS**

Consider this an after-dinner coffee, hot chocolate, and decadent dessert all rolled into one.

CRUST
- ½ cup all-purpose flour
- ⅓ cup granulated sugar
- ¼ tsp. kosher salt
- 3 Tbsp. Dutch-process cocoa powder
- 3 Tbsp. chilled butter, cut into ½-inch cubes
- 1 large egg yolk
- 1 Tbsp. heavy whipping cream

FILLING
- 1 pt. coffee ice cream, softened
- ½ pt. chocolate ice cream (1 cup), softened
- Store-bought caramel sauce
- Whipped cream
- Cocoa nibs or chocolate-covered espresso beans, for serving (optional)

1. Prepare Crust: In a food processor, pulse flour, sugar, salt, and cocoa to combine. Add butter; pulse until mixture resembles coarse meal with some pea-size pieces remaining. Stir together yolk and cream; drizzle over flour mixture, pulsing several times to combine. Transfer mixture to a 9-inch fluted tart pan with a removable bottom, pressing evenly into bottom and up sides. Refrigerate until firm, about 20 minutes.

2. Preheat oven to 350°F. Prick bottom of crust at 1-inch intervals with the tines of a fork. Bake in preheated oven until set and dry, about 15 minutes. Let cool completely on a wire rack.

3. Prepare Filling: Stir together softened coffee ice cream and chocolate ice cream in a large bowl until no streaks remain; transfer to cooled crust, spreading all the way to edges and smoothing top with an offset spatula. Freeze until firm, about 1 hour (or wrap in plastic and freeze up to 1 week).

4. Remove tart from pan. Drizzle with caramel. Spoon whipped cream on top and drizzle with more caramel. Sprinkle with cocoa nibs or decorate with chocolate espresso beans. Cut into wedges, dipping knife blade in hot water and wiping clean between each cut to ensure clean slices.

Go Dutch!

Dutch-process cocoa powder has been treated with an alkalizing agent to decrease its acidity, making it both darker and less bitter. It lends a more intense chocolate flavor and deeper color, while natural cocoa (the term for non-'Dutched' cocoa powders) results in both a lighter color and a sharp, more acidic flavor.

SHARE
gifts from the kitchen

Sunny Delights

Cool-season citrus takes center stage in these juicy, sweet-tart treats tailor-made for giving.

recipes

Clementine-Vanilla Bean Marmalade
Spiced Orange-Roll Coffee Cake
Cranberry-Orange Shortbread Cookies
Pistachio-Lemon Bars

Clementine-Vanilla Bean Marmalade

MAKES **6 CUPS** • ACTIVE **30 MIN.** • TOTAL **2 HOURS, 15 MIN., PLUS 24 HOURS CHILLING AND COOLING**

It's peak season for these juicy, easy-to-peel citrus fruits. (Hint: The smaller the size, the sweeter they are.) Buy a bag or box, and use them to make an edible gift to brighten anyone's day.

- 3 lb. seedless clementines (mandarin oranges)
- 2 lemons
- 3 Tbsp. minced crystallized ginger
- ½ tsp. kosher salt
- 4½ cups granulated sugar
- 2 tsp. vanilla bean paste

1. Slice ends off clementines and lemons. Slice each piece of fruit in half from end to end. Thinly slice each half into ¼-inch-thick half-moons. Cut each half-moon in half so every piece is a quarter of a slice. Discard lemon seeds. Bring clementines, lemons, and 6 cups water to a boil in a large Dutch oven over medium-high. Reduce heat to medium, and simmer 5 minutes. Remove from heat; let stand 30 minutes. Cover; chill 12 to 24 hours.

2. Prepare a boiling water canner. Heat 6 half-pint glass jars in simmering water until ready to use. Do not boil. Wash lids in soapy water, and set bands aside.

3. Uncover clementine mixture; bring to a simmer over medium. Stir in ginger and salt. Cook, stirring occasionally, until citrus rinds are very soft, about 30 minutes.

4. Stir in sugar and vanilla bean paste. Bring mixture to a boil over medium-high. Reduce heat to medium; attach a candy thermometer to side of Dutch oven. Cook, stirring every 3 to 4 minutes, until thermometer registers 220°F, about 45 minutes. (A spoon dragged across bottom of pot should briefly leave a clean line.)

5. Remove mixture from heat; carefully ladle into hot sterilized jars, filling to ¼ inch from top. Remove air bubbles; wipe jar rims. Center lids on jars, and apply bands. Adjust to fingertip tight. Lower jars into boiling water canner, and process, covered, for 10 minutes. Turn off heat, uncover, and let jars stand 5 minutes. Remove jars from canner; cool 12 to 24 hours. Check lids for seal. (Lids should not flex when center is pressed.) Store in a cool, dark, dry place up to 18 months. Or, store unprocessed marmalade in airtight jars in the refrigerator up to 1 month.

Spiced Orange-Roll Coffee Cake

SERVES 12 • ACTIVE 25 MIN. • TOTAL 1 HOUR, 30 MIN., PLUS 2 HOURS COOLING

Serve this lightly spiced orange cake for breakfast or dessert.

- 3¾ cups bleached cake flour, divided, plus more for pan
- 1½ cups packed light brown sugar, divided
- 2⅛ tsp. orange zest plus 1 to 2 Tbsp. fresh juice (from 2 navel oranges), divided
- 1½ tsp. kosher salt, divided
- ½ tsp. pumpkin pie spice, divided
- 1 cup unsalted butter, softened and divided, plus more for greasing pan
- 1 cup granulated sugar
- 10 oz. cream cheese, softened and divided
- 4 large eggs
- 1 tsp. vanilla extract
- 2 tsp. baking powder
- ¼ tsp. baking soda
- ¼ cup powdered sugar

1. Combine 1¼ cups of the flour, 1 cup of the brown sugar, 1 teaspoon of the zest, 1 teaspoon of the salt, and ¼ teaspoon of the pumpkin pie spice in a bowl. Place ¼ cup of the butter in a microwavable dish; microwave on HIGH until melted, about 30 seconds. Add to flour mixture; stir until crumbles form. Chill, covered, until ready to use.

2. Preheat oven to 350°F. Lightly grease a 10-inch tube pan with butter, and dust with flour; set aside. Stir together granulated sugar, 1 teaspoon of the zest, and remaining ½ cup brown sugar in a medium bowl, rubbing zest and sugars between your fingers; set aside. Beat 8 ounces of the cream cheese and remaining ¾ cup butter in bowl of a stand mixer fitted with a paddle attachment on medium until smooth, about 1 minute. Add sugar mixture to cream cheese mixture, and beat on medium until light and fluffy, about 4 minutes. Add eggs, 1 at a time, beating well after each addition, scraping down sides of bowl as needed. Beat in vanilla until combined.

3. Stir together baking powder, baking soda, and remaining 2½ cups flour, ½ teaspoon salt, and ¼ teaspoon pumpkin pie spice in a bowl. Gradually add flour mixture to cream cheese mixture, beating on low until combined, about 2 minutes. Spoon half of batter into prepared pan, spreading in an even layer. Top with half of reserved crumble mixture. Repeat layers once with remaining batter and crumble mixture.

4. Bake in preheated oven until a wooden pick inserted in center comes out clean, 50 to 55 minutes, tenting with aluminum foil after 35 minutes. Cool cake in pan on a wire rack for 15 minutes. Invert onto a plate; invert again onto wire rack, crumble side up. Let cool completely, about 2 hours.

5. Beat powdered sugar, 1 tablespoon of the orange juice, and remaining ⅛ teaspoon zest and 2 ounces cream cheese with an electric mixer on medium until smooth, about 1 minute. Add up to remaining 1 tablespoon orange juice, 1 teaspoon at a time, until desired consistency is reached. Drizzle glaze over cooled cake as desired.

Pro Tip: A distant cousin of cinnamon buns, the zesty glazed pastries make an appearance at nearly every gathering the same way coffee cakes do in my hometown in South Georgia. Both are sweet enough to be served for dessert but not so sugary that they're banned from breakfast. My Orange-Roll Coffee Cake combines the two—it's a hug from my past and a celebration of my present in a way that's comforting yet new. That's what I love about being a Southerner: Certain foods ground us and make us feel at home, no matter where we are.
— *Ivy Odom,* Southern Living *Senior Lifestyle Producer*

Cranberry-Orange Shortbread Cookies

MAKES **ABOUT 2 DOZEN** • ACTIVE **30 MIN.** • TOTAL **45 MIN., PLUS 2 HOURS CHILLING**

Tangy orange and chewy dried cranberries are delicious counterpoints to the richness of buttery shortbread.

- **1 cup butter, softened**
- **¾ cup granulated sugar**
- **2 large eggs**
- **1 tsp. vanilla extract**
- **2 tsp. orange zest**
- **2½ cups all-purpose flour**
- **½ tsp. baking soda**
- **½ tsp. kosher salt**
- **¼ cup cornstarch**
- **⅓ cup chopped dried cranberries, plus more for garnish**
- **Vanilla- or white chocolate-flavor melting wafers**

1. Beat butter and sugar in a large bowl with an electric mixer on medium until light and fluffy. Beat in eggs, vanilla extract, and orange zest.

2. In another bowl, combine flour, baking powder, salt, and cornstarch; gradually add to butter mixture with cranberries, beating on low until combined. Shape dough into a disk; wrap in plastic wrap. Chill 2 hours.

3. Roll dough on a floured surface into a ½-inch-thick square; cut into 3-inch rectangles. Bake until firm and lightly golden around the edges, about 18 minutes. Let cool in pan on a wire rack 5 minutes. Transfer to a rack to cool completely.

4. Melt melting wafers according to package directions. Dip cooled cookies into melted candy coating; top with additional dried cranberries.

Pistachio-Lemon Bars

MAKES **16** • ACTIVE **20 MIN.** • TOTAL **1 HOUR, 10 MIN., PLUS 1 HOUR, 30 MIN. CHILLING**

Wipe the knife's blade with a damp paper towel after each slice for the neatest bars.

Nonstick cooking spray

1½ cups all-purpose flour, divided

1 cup granulated sugar, divided

½ cup butter, cubed and softened

¼ tsp. kosher salt

6 large eggs, at room temperature

1 cup fresh lemon juice (from 6 large lemons)

2 Tbsp. lemon zest, divided

¼ cup chopped salted pistachios

Powdered sugar, for dusting

1. Preheat oven to 350°F with rack in center position. Lightly coat an 8-inch square baking pan with cooking spray; line bottom and sides with parchment paper, leaving a 1-inch overhang.

2. Stir together 1 cup of the flour and ¼ cup of the granulated sugar in a medium bowl. Add butter. Work butter into flour mixture, using your fingers, until a shaggy dough forms and no large chunks remain, about 1 minute. (Mixture should hold together when squeezed.) Press evenly into bottom and about ½ inch up sides of prepared pan. Bake, uncovered, in preheated oven until lightly browned, 20 to 25 minutes.

3. Meanwhile, whisk together remaining ½ cup flour, remaining ¾ cup granulated sugar, and salt in a large bowl. Add eggs and lemon juice, whisking mixture just until combined. Pour through a fine-mesh strainer into a large bowl, using a spatula to press mixture through strainer. Discard solids. Whisk in 1 tablespoon of the lemon zest.

4. Reduce oven temperature to 300°F. Carefully pour filling over crust. Bake, uncovered, until filling is set around edges and jiggles slightly in center, 20 to 25 minutes.

5. Transfer to a wire rack, and let cool 20 minutes. Cover with plastic wrap, and refrigerate until filling is completely set, 1 hour, 30 minutes to 3 hours.

6. Carefully lift up and out of baking pan, using parchment paper as handles. Transfer to a cutting board. Cut into squares. Sprinkle lemon bars with remaining 1 tablespoon lemon zest and chopped pistachios. Just before serving, use a fine-mesh strainer to dust with powdered sugar.

Thanks

Thanks to the following shops, vendors, and artisans whose products were featured on the pages of this book and to the many we may have not listed here:

Accent Décor	**Hall's Birmingham Wholesale Florist**	**Pomegranate**
A'mano		**Sarah Thorne Art**
Anthropologie	**Hobby Lobby**	**Sexton's Seafood**
Aspen & Arlo	**Houses and Parties**	**Shoppe**
Astier de Villatte	**JSH Home Essentials**	**Son of a Butcher**
BC Clark	**Leaf & Petal**	**Sooner Wholesale Florist**
Bradford House Hotel	**Lion Ribbon**	**Stout Textiles**
Bromberg's	**Maison Venu**	**Target**
Christmas Expressions	**Marbled Paper Studio**	**Terrain**
Davis Wholesale Florist	**Mottahedeh**	**Trader Joe's**
Etsy	**OKC Floral Market**	**Whole Foods Market**
Fenwick Fields	**Park Hill Collection**	**Willow Park Boutique**
	Pastiche Studios	

Thanks to the following individuals for allowing us into their homes to decorate and photograph:

Sidney and Matt Bragiel

Mindy and Paul Brown

Sarah Kate and Jason Little

Nikki Pratt

Sara Gae and Greg Waters

General Index

A
A Little Christmas, 28–39
acorns, gilded, 34
activities, record of, 190
amaryllis, 46–49
anemones, 15, 24
apples, decorating with, 46–49
artisans, list of, 168

B
boxwood, 183
Bring In the Greens, 127
Brussels sprouts, storing, 131

C
cast-iron pans, 122
cedar, 183
Centerpieces
    citrus and greenery, 45
    low, with hypericum, 17
    quick, 179
    roses, peonies, and anemones, 15
chandeliers, 15, 16, 25
Christmas card list, 189
Christmas Dinner Planner, 186-187
Christmas songs
    'O Christmas Tree', 22
    'We Need a Little Christmas', 32
citrus fruits, drying, 45
clementine topiary, 42–43
Cooking tips
    Brussels sprouts, storing, 131
    cast-iron pans, 122
    green beans, trimming, 75
    ham hocks, about, 125
    slow cooker's warm setting, 118
cypress, 27

D
December calendar, 180–181
Decorating Planner, 182
Decorations, handmade
    acorns, gilded, 34
    clementine topiary, 42–43
    gold foil sheets, 34
    seed pods, gilded, 34
decorator's toolkit, 182
Dining room
    nontraditional colors, 14–15
    pink and green, 16–17
    round tables, 18–19
Dish Up Good Luck, 90–103
drying citrus, 45

E
eucalyptus, 24, 183

F
Festive Fruits, 40–53
fir branches, 183
Floral arrangements
    anemones and plumosa, 24
    greenery-topped trays, 24
Frosty Favorites, 146–155
fruit and spice potpourri, 49

G
Gambrel, Steven, 38–39
Garlands
    ceiling, 30–31
    evergreen and citrus, 42–43
gift list, 188
gift tags, 37
gift wrapping station, 37
gifts from the kitchen, 156–167
gilded decorations, 34–35
gold foil sheets, 34
green beans, trimming, 75
greenery for decorations, 183

H
ham hocks, about, 125
Hepburn, Audrey, 36
Holiday Planner, 177–192
homeowners, list of, 168
hotlines, holiday, 179
hypericum berries, 17, 43

J
juniper, 183

K
Kaleidoscope Christmas, 12–27

L
lemon cypress tree, 46
Lists
    activities, 190
    cards, 189
    decorating, 182
    gifts, 188
    ideas for next year, 192
    recipes, favorite, 191
    thank-you notes, 192
    traditions, 190
    visits and visitors, 191
Little, Jason, 29
Little, Sarah Kate, 29

M

magnolia, 183
Main Pleasers, 116–125
Mantels, decorating
    asparagus fern, with, 20–21
    stockings, 20–21
McMurry, Leonard D., 27
memories, record of, 190–191
Menus
    Dish Up Good Luck, 91
    Relish the Feast, 67
    Serve Up Good Cheer, 57
metric equivalents, 172
Mother Teresa, 47

N

Next Year, Notes for, 192
November calendar, 178–179

O

'O Christmas Tree, 22
Odom, Ivy, 163
olive branches, 183
oranges, dried, 42–43
oranges studded with cloves, 45
Ornaments
    dried pear, 52
    gilded, 34
    wicker bells, 17
Outdoor decorating
    front porch, 12
    greenery on statues, 27

P

Party Dressing, 136–145
Party Planner, 184–185
pears, decorating with, 50–53
peonies, 15
pepper berry, 27
pine branches, 15, 183
Pink Cockatrice plates, 17
place cards, 181
Place settings
    with wicker bells, 17
place-card holders, pears for, 50–51
Planners
    Christmas dinner, 186–187
    decorating, 182
    party, 184–185
plates, Pink Cockatrice, 17
plumosa, 24
poinsettia, 24
potpourri, fruit and spice, 49

Q

Quotes
    Hepburn, Audrey, 36
    Mother Teresa, 47
    'O Christmas Tree', 22
    'We Need a Little Christmas', 32

R

Relish the Feast, 66–79
Ribbons
    taffeta, 48–49
    wall hangings, on, 21
roses, 15

S

seed pods, gold-painted, 34
Serve Up Good Cheer, 56–65
shops, list of, 168
side board, Louis XVI, 38–39
slow cooker's warm setting, 118
Sunny Delights, 158–167

T

Take a Dip, 106–115
thank-you note checklist, 192
Topiary
    clementine, 42–43
    pear, 52–53
Trees
    fir, 23
    flocked, 23
    lemon cypress, 46–47

V

vases, French wedding, 37
vendors, list of, 168

W

We Need a Little Christmas, 32
Whip Up Sweet Surprises, 80–89
wicker bells, 17
Wreaths
    with berries and apples, 48–49
    dried oranges, 42–43
window, with satin bows, 15
writing desk, 37

Metric Charts

The recipes that appear in this cookbook use the standard US method for measuring liquid and dry or solid ingredients (teaspoons, tablespoons, and cups). The information on these pages is provided to help cooks outside the United States successfully use these recipes. All equivalents are approximate.

Metric Equivalents for Different Types of Ingredients

A standard cup measure of a dry or solid ingredient will vary in weight depending on the type of ingredient. A standard cup of liquid is the same volume for any type of liquid. Use the following chart when converting standard cup measures to grams (weight) or milliliters (volume).

STANDARD CUP	FINE POWDER (ex. flour)	GRAIN (ex. rice)	GRANULAR (ex. sugar)	LIQUID SOLIDS (ex. butter)	LIQUID (ex. milk)
1	140 g	150 g	190 g	200 g	240 ml
¾	105 g	113 g	143 g	150 g	180 ml
⅔	93 g	100 g	125 g	133 g	160 ml
½	70 g	75 g	95 g	100 g	120 ml
⅓	47 g	50 g	63 g	67 g	80 ml
¼	35 g	38 g	48 g	50 g	60 ml
⅛	18 g	19 g	24 g	25 g	30 ml

Useful Equivalents for Liquid Ingredients by Volume

TSP	TBSP	CUPS	FL OZ	ML	L
¼ tsp				1 ml	
½ tsp				2 ml	
1 tsp				5 ml	
3 tsp	1 Tbsp		½ fl oz	15 ml	
	2 Tbsp	⅛ cup	1 fl oz	30 ml	
	4 Tbsp	¼ cup	2 fl oz	60 ml	
	5⅓ Tbsp	⅓ cup	3 fl oz	80 ml	
	8 Tbsp	½ cup	4 fl oz	120 ml	
	10⅔ Tbsp	⅔ cup	5 fl oz	160 ml	
	12 Tbsp	¾ cup	6 fl oz	180 ml	
	16 Tbsp	1 cup	8 fl oz	240 ml	
	1 pt	2 cups	16 fl oz	480 ml	
	1 qt	4 cups	32 fl oz	960 ml	
			33 fl oz	1000 ml	1 L

Useful Equivalents for Dry Ingredients by Weight

(To convert ounces to grams, multiply the number of ounces by 30.)

OZ	LB	G
1 oz	¹⁄₁₆ lb	30 g
4 oz	¼ lb	120 g
8 oz	½ lb	240 g
12 oz	¾ lb	360 g
16 oz	1 lb	480 g

Useful Equivalents for Length

(To convert inches to centimeters, multiply the number of inches by 2.5.)

IN	FT	YD	CM	M
1 in			2.5 cm	
6 in	½ ft		15 cm	
12 in	1 ft		30 cm	
36 in	3 ft	1 yd	90 cm	
40 in			100 cm	1 m

Useful Equivalents for Cooking/Oven Temperatures

	FAHRENHEIT	CELSIUS	GAS MARK
FREEZE WATER	32°F	0°C	
ROOM TEMPERATURE	68°F	20°C	
BOIL WATER	212°F	100°C	
	325°F	160°C	3
	350°F	180°C	4
	375°F	190°C	5
	400°F	200°C	6
	425°F	220°C	7
	450°F	230°C	8
BROIL			Grill

Recipe Index

A
Almonds
    Almond "Surprise" Cakes, 103
    Green Beans with Garlic Vinaigrette, 75
Appetizers and snacks. See also Dips and spreads
    Cheesy Caramelized Onion Flatbreads, 63
    Gorgonzola Cheesecake with Pear Preserves and Pecans, 115
    Mini Beef Wellingtons, 62
    Okra in a Blanket, 63
    Pickled Beets, 71
    Roquefort-Cognac Cheese Spread, 71
    Smoked Salmon Mousse Canapés, 62
    The Southern Relish Tray, 70–71
    Warm Olives with Citrus Zest, 70
    Zesty Pickled Roots, 70
Apples
    Fennel-and-Fruit Wild Rice Dressing, 142
    Mulled-Cider Cranberry Relish, 72
    Pork Roast with Apples, Bacon, and Cabbage, 121
Asparagus with Cheese Sauce and Breadcrumbs, 128

B
Bacon
    Classic Hoppin' John, 100
    Coq au Vin, 122
    Cornbread Dressing with Green Chile and Chorizo, 141
    Pork Roast with Apples, Bacon, and Cabbage, 121
Beans & Rice, Monday Red, 125
Beef
    Mini Beef Wellingtons, 62
    Pumpernickel Roast Beef, 118
Beer
    Beer-Cheese Fondue, 108
    Pork Roast with Apples, Bacon, and Cabbage, 121
    Pumpernickel Roast Beef, 118
Beets, Pickled, 71
Beverages
    Grapefruit, Rosemary, and Sage Sparkler, 58
    Paper Plane Cocktail, 68
    Prosperity Punch, 92
Biscuits, Cornmeal-Chive, 100
Boiled Shrimp, 111
Bourbon
    Bourbon-Chocolate Baby Bombes, 65
    Bourbon Ganache, 65
    Eggnog Baked Alaska, 148
    Paper Plane Cocktail, 68

Brandy
    Prosperity Punch, 92
    Roquefort-Cognac Cheese Spread, 71
    Tipsy Strawberry Truffles, 83
Broccoli
    Floret Medley with Cheese Straw Crumbs, 132
Brown Butter Cornbread, 138
Brown Butter Cornbread Dressing, 138
Brussels Sprouts with Maple Syrup and Pecans, 131

C
Cabbage
    Confetti Chow Chow, 95
    Pork Roast with Apples, Bacon, and Cabbage, 121
Cakes
    Almond "Surprise" Cakes, 103
    Bourbon Chocolate Baby Bombes, 65
    Spiced Orange-Roll Coffee Cake, 163
    Vanilla Layer Cake with Fruit-and-Herb Wreath, 79
Candy
    Cappuccino-Walnut Toffee, 88
    Creamy Strawberry-Vanilla Bean Truffles, 83
    Fresh Strawberry Truffles, 83
    Strawberry-Coconut Truffles, 83
    Tipsy Strawberry Truffles, 83
Cappuccino-Walnut Toffee, 88
Carrots
    Coq au Vin, 122
    Zesty Pickled Roots, 70
Cauliflower
    Floret Medley with Cheese Straw Crumbs, 132
Celery
    Good-Fortune Fish Dip, 95
    Roquefort-Cognac Cheese Spread, 71
    Savory Mushroom and Herb Dressing, 145
Cheese. See also Cream cheese
    Asparagus with Cheese Sauce and Breadcrumbs, 128
    Beer-Cheese Fondue, 108
    Cheesy Caramelized Onion Flatbreads, 63
    Clementine-and-Collard Salad with Pomegranate Seeds, 96
    Creamed Greens with Garlic Crust, 135
    Gorgonzola Cheesecake with Pear Preserves and Pecans, 115
    Mini Beef Wellingtons, 62
    Roquefort-Cognac Cheese Spread, 71
    Two-Potato Gratin, 75
    Warm Gumbo Dip, 112
Cheese Straw Crumbs, 132
Cherries-and-Cream Icebox Cake, 151

Chocolate. See also White chocolate
    Bourbon-Chocolate Baby Bombes, 65
    Bourbon Ganache, 65
    Cappuccino-Walnut Toffee, 88
    Chocolate-Peppermint Thumbprints, 84
    Frozen Café-Mocha Tart, 155
    Hot Fudge, 152
    Red Velvet-White Chocolate Cookies, 87
    Turtle Sundaes, 152
Chow Chow, Confetti, 95
Classic Hoppin' John, 100
Classic Rémoulade with Boiled Shrimp, 111
Clementine-and-Collard Salad with Pomegranate Seeds, 96
Clementine-Vanilla Bean Marmalade, 160
Coconut-Strawberry Truffles, 83
Coffee
    Bourbon Chocolate Baby Bombes, 65
    Cappuccino-Walnut Toffee, 88
    Frozen Café-Mocha Tart, 155
Confetti Chow Chow, 95
Cookies and bars
    Chocolate-Peppermint Thumbprints, 84
    Cranberry Shortbread Bars, 88
    Cranberry-Orange Shortbread Cookies, 164
    Maple-Gingerbread People, 84
    Pistachio-Lemon Bars, 167
    Red Velvet-White Chocolate Cookies, 87
    Snowflake Sugar Cookies, 87
Coq au Vin, 122
Cornbread Dressing with Green Chile and Chorizo, 141
Cornmeal
    Brown Butter Cornbread, 138
    Cornmeal-Chive Biscuits, 100
Cranberries
    Cranberry Shortbread Bars, 88
    Cranberry-Orange Shortbread Cookies, 164
    Mulled-Cider Cranberry Relish, 72
Cream cheese
    Cherries-and-Cream Icebox Cake, 151
    Creamed Greens with Garlic Crust, 135
    Good-Fortune Fish Dip, 95
    Gorgonzola Cheesecake with Pear Preserves and Pecans, 115
    Roquefort-Cognac Cheese Spread, 71
    Smoked Salmon Mousse Canapés, 62
    Spiced Orange-Roll Coffee Cake, 163
    Warm Gumbo Dip, 112
Creamed Greens with Garlic Crust, 135
Creamy Strawberry-Vanilla Bean Truffles, 83
Cucumbers
    Smoked Salmon Mousse Canapés, 62

D

Desserts. See also Cakes; Candy; Cookies and bars
- Cherries-and-Cream Icebox Cake, 151
- Eggnog Baked Alaska, 148
- Frozen Café-Mocha Tart, 155
- Turtle Sundaes, 152

Dips and spreads
- Beer-Cheese Fondue, 108
- Classic Rémoulade with Boiled Shrimp, 111
- Good-Fortune Fish Dip, 95
- Gorgonzola Cheesecake with Pear Preserves and Pecans, 115
- Preserved Lemon Labneh Dip, 108
- Warm Gumbo Dip, 112

Dressings
- Brown Butter Cornbread Dressing, 138
- Cornbread Dressing with Green Chile and Chorizo, 141
- Fennel-and-Fruit Wild Rice Dressing, 142
- Savory Mushroom and Herb Dressing, 145

Dry-Brined Turkey with Pecan Gremolata, 76

E

Eggnog Baked Alaska, 148

F

Fennel-and-Fruit Wild Rice Dressing, 142

Fish and shellfish
- Boiled Shrimp, 111
- Classic Rémoulade with Boiled Shrimp, 111
- Good-Fortune Fish Dip, 95
- Smoked Salmon Mousse Canapés, 62

Flatbreads, Cheesy Caramelized Onion, 63
Floret Medley with Cheese Straw Crumbs, 132
Fresh Strawberry Truffles, 83

Frostings and icings
- Bourbon Ganache, 65
- Royal Icing, 84
- Vanilla Buttercream, 79

Frozen Café-Mocha Tart, 155

G

Garlic
- Creamed Greens with Garlic Crust, 135
- Dry-Brined Turkey with Pecan Gremolata, 76
- Green Beans with Garlic Vinaigrette, 75
- Pecan Gremolata, 76

Good-Fortune Fish Dip, 95
Gorgonzola Cheesecake with Pear Preserves and Pecans, 115
Grapefruit, Rosemary, and Sage Sparkler, 58

Grapes
- Ice Ring, 92
- Prosperity Punch, 92

Green Beans with Garlic Vinaigrette, 75

Greens
- Clementine-and-Collard Salad with Pomegranate Seeds, 96
- Creamed Greens with Garlic Crust, 135
- Pomegranate, Pear, and Arugula Salad, 72

Gremolata, Pecan, 76

H

Ham. See Pork
Homemade Labneh, 108
Hoppin' John, Classic, 100
Hot Fudge, 152

I

Ice Ring, 92

L

Lemon(s)
- Asparagus with Cheese Sauce and Breadcrumbs, 128
- Boiled Shrimp, 111
- Clementine-Vanilla Bean Marmalade, 160
- Fresh Strawberry Truffles, 83
- Good-Fortune Fish Dip, 95
- Green Beans with Garlic Vinaigrette, 75
- Ice Ring, 92
- Pecan Gremolata, 76
- Pistachio-Lemon Bars, 167
- Pomegranate, Pear, and Arugula Salad, 72
- Preserved Lemon Labneh Dip, 108
- Prosperity Punch, 92
- Warm Olives with Citrus Zest, 70

M

Maple-Gingerbread People, 84
Marmalade, Clementine-Vanilla Bean, 160
Mini Beef Wellingtons, 62
Monday Red Beans & Rice, 125
Mulled Cider-Cranberry Relish, 72

Mushrooms
- Coq au Vin, 122
- Mini Beef Wellingtons, 62
- Savory Mushroom and Herb Dressing, 145

O

Okra
- Okra in a Blanket, 63
- Warm Gumbo Dip, 112

Old Bay Your Way, 111
Olives with Citrus Zest, Warm, 70

Onions
- Cheesy Caramelized Onion Flatbreads, 63
- Pickled Beets, 71
- Pork Roast with Apples, Bacon, and Cabbage, 121
- Pumpernickel Roast Beef, 118

Orange(s)
- Almond "Surprise" Cakes, 103
- Clementine-and-Collard Salad with Pomegranate Seeds, 96
- Clementine-Vanilla Bean Marmalade, 160
- Cranberry-Orange Shortbread Cookies, 164
- Maple-Gingerbread People, 84
- Mulled-Cider Cranberry Relish, 72
- Paper Plane Cocktail, 68
- Pomegranate, Pear, and Arugula Salad, 72
- Spiced Orange-Roll Coffee Cake, 163
- Warm Olives with Citrus Zest, 70

P

Paper Plane Cocktail, 68

Parsnips
- Zesty Pickled Roots, 70

Pears
- Gorgonzola Cheesecake with Pear Preserves and Pecans, 115
- Pomegranate, Pear, and Arugula Salad, 72

Pecans
- Bourbon-Chocolate Baby Bombes, 65
- Brussels Sprouts with Maple Syrup and Pecans, 131
- Clementine-and-Collard Salad with Pomegranate Seeds, 96
- Gorgonzola Cheesecake with Pear Preserves and Pecans, 115
- Pecan Gremolata, 76
- Turtle Sundaes, 152

Pepper Jelly and Ginger Glazed Ham, 101
Peppermint-Chocolate Thumbprints, 84
Peppers, bell
    Classic Hoppin' John, 100
    Confetti Chow Chow, 95
    Monday Red Beans & Rice, 125
    Warm Gumbo Dip, 112
Peppers, chile
    Confetti Chow Chow, 95
    Cornbread Dressing with Green Chile and Chorizo, 141
Pickled Beets, 71
Pistachio-Lemon Bars, 167
Pomegranate
    Almond "Surprise" Cakes, 103
    Clementine-and-Collard Salad with Pomegranate Seeds, 96
    Pomegranate, Pear, and Arugula Salad, 72
    Vanilla Layer Cake with Fruit-and-Herb Wreath, 79
Pork. See also Bacon; Sausages
    Monday Red Beans & Rice, 125
    Okra in a Blanket, 63
    Pepper Jelly and Ginger Glazed Ham, 101
    Pork Roast with Apples, Bacon, and Cabbage, 121
Potato Gratin, Two-, 75
Poultry
    Coq au Vin, 122
    Dry-Brined Turkey with Pecan Gremolata, 76
Preserved Lemon Labneh Dip, 108
Prosperity Punch, 92
Pumpernickel Roast Beef, 118

R
Radishes
    Zesty Pickled Roots, 70
Red Velvet–White Chocolate Cookies, 87
Relish, Mulled-Cider Cranberry, 72
Rice
    Classic Hoppin' John, 100
    Fennel-and-Fruit Wild Rice Dressing, 142
    Monday Red Beans & Rice, 125
Roquefort-Cognac Cheese Spread, 71
Royal Icing, 84

S
Salads
    Clementine-and-Collard Salad with Pomegranate Seeds, 96
    Pomegranate, Pear, and Arugula Salad, 72
Sausages
    Cornbread Dressing with Green Chile and Chorizo, 141
    Monday Red Beans & Rice, 125
    Savory Mushroom and Herb Dressing, 145
    Warm Gumbo Dip, 112
Savory Mushroom and Herb Dressing, 145
Shallots
    Brussels Sprouts with Maple Syrup and Pecans, 131
    Classic Rémoulade with Boiled Shrimp, 111
    Clementine-and-Collard Salad with Pomegranate Seeds, 96
    Pomegranate, Pear, and Arugula Salad, 72
Shrimp. See Fish and shellfish
Slow-cooker recipes
    Pork Roast with Apples, Bacon, and Cabbage, 121
    Pumpernickel Roast Beef, 118
    Smoked Salmon Mousse Canapés, 62
    Snowflake Sugar Cookies, 87
    Southern Relish Tray, The, 70–71
    Spiced Orange-Roll Coffee Cake, 163
Strawberries
    Creamy Strawberry-Vanilla Bean Truffles, 83
    Fresh Strawberry Truffles, 83
    Strawberry-Coconut Truffles, 83
    Tipsy Strawberry Truffles, 83
Swiss Meringue, 148

T
Tipsy Strawberry Truffles, 83
Tomatoes
    Confetti Chow Chow, 95
    Cornbread Dressing with Green Chile and Chorizo, 141
Turnips
    Zesty Pickled Roots, 70
Turtle Sundaes, 152
Two-Potato Gratin, 75

V
Vanilla Buttercream, 79
Vanilla Layer Cake with Fruit-and-Herb Wreath, 79

W
Walnuts
    Cappuccino-Walnut Toffee, 88
    Fennel-and-Fruit Wild Rice Dressing, 142
    Gorgonzola Cheesecake with Pear Preserves and Pecans, 115
Warm Gumbo Dip, 112
Warm Olives with Citrus Zest, 70
White chocolate
    Cappuccino-Walnut Toffee, 88
    Cranberry-Orange Shortbread Cookies, 164
    Creamy Strawberry-Vanilla Bean Truffles, 83
    Fresh Strawberry Truffles, 83
    Red Velvet–White Chocolate Cookies, 87
    Strawberry-Coconut Truffles, 83
    Tipsy Strawberry Truffles, 83
Wine
    Boiled Shrimp, 111
    Coq au Vin, 122
    Pepper Jelly and Ginger Glazed Ham, 101
    Prosperity Punch, 92

Y
Yogurt
    Homemade Labneh, 108
    Preserved Lemon Labneh Dip, 108

Z
Zesty Pickled Roots, 70

©2025 Southern Living Books, a division of Meredith Operations Corporation
225 Liberty Street, New York, NY 10281

Southern Living is a trademark of TI Inc. Lifestyle Group LLC, a subsidiary of Meredith Operations Corporation, registered in the U.S. and other countries. All rights reserved. No part of this book may be reproduced in any form or by any means without the prior written permission of the publisher, excepting brief quotations in connection with reviews written specifically for inclusion in magazines or newspapers, or limited excerpts strictly for personal use.

DOTDASH MEREDITH CONSUMER MARKETING
Director, Direct Marketing-Books: Daniel Fagan
Marketing Operations Manager: Max Daily
Marketing Manager: Kylie Dazzo
Senior Marketing Coordinator: Elizabeth Moore
Content Manager: Julie Doll
Senior Production Manager: Liza Ward

PRODUCED BY:
BLUELINE CREATIVE GROUP LLC
visit: bluelinecreativegroup.com
Producer/Editor: Katherine Cobbs
Book Designer: Claire Cormany

LOCATION PHOTOGRAPHY:
Location Photographers: Caitlin Bensel, Emily Hart
Location Photographer's Assistant: Laura Evans
Location Stylists: Sidney Bragiel, Katherine Cobbs, Sara Gae Waters

STUDIO PHOTOGRAPHY:
Photographer: Caitlin Bensel
Prop Stylist: Sidney Bragiel
Prop Stylist's Assistant: Tucker Vines
Food Stylist: Torie Cox
Food Stylist's Assistants: Sally McKay, Kady Wohlfarth

PRINT PRODUCTION:
WATERBURY PUBLICATIONS, INC.

A Library of Congress control number has been applied for.

ISBN-13: 978-1-4197-8813-0

First Edition 2025
Printed in the United States of America
10 9 8 7 6 5 4 3 2 1
Call 1-800-826-4707 for more information

Distributed in 2025 by Abrams, an imprint of ABRAMS.
Abrams® is a registered trademark of Harry N. Abrams, Inc.

ABRAMS The Art of Books
195 Broadway, New York, NY 10007
abramsbooks.com

Holiday Planner

Simplify the holiday season and keep your spirits bright with our helpful planner. Manage guest lists, keep tabs on gifts for family and friends, and stay on top of all of your holiday to-dos so that your Christmas season is the merriest of all.

Planning Calendar for November
Centerpieces in Seconds
Planning Calendar for December
Place Card Panache
Decorating Planner
Party Planner
Christmas Dinner Planner
Gifts & Greetings
Holiday Memories
Looking Ahead

November 2025 *daily to-dos:*

SUNDAY	MONDAY	TUESDAY	WEDNESDAY
Daylight saving time ends. Turn your clocks back one hour at 2 a.m. You'll need the extra hour of rest for the holiday rush! **2**	Set out woodsy or spice-scented candles to awaken the holiday spirit. **3**	Draw up a preholiday to-do list. Delegate chores, and cross off items as you accomplish them. **4**	If you're planning to prepare a fresh, not frozen, Thanksgiving turkey, order it now. **5**
Plan your centerpiece. Pre-order any flowers or greenery you might need. **9**	Purchase your holiday cards. Save time and choose a company that can print, address, stamp, and mail them. **10**	Follow up with any guests who have not yet RSVP'd to Thanksgiving dinner. A final head count makes menu planning easier. **11**	Will you need separate seating for kids? Designate a small table. Buy craft paper to cover it, and get crayons for the little ones. **12**
Round up board games, playing cards, and family photo albums to have on hand to keep Thanksgiving guests entertained while you're busy in the kitchen. **16**	Iron linens you plan to use on the holiday table. Now's also the time to polish silver if needed. **17**	Make a menu prep list. Draw up a daily plan through Thanksgiving Day to spread tasks out as much as possible. TIP: Did you know you can make cranberry sauce up to three weeks ahead and freeze it? **18**	Shop for perishable grocery items like milk, cheese, and produce. **19**
Baking a holiday pie? Ensure you've got what you need. **23**	Purchase fresh flowers and any other perishable items needed for your centerpiece, then assemble it. **24**	Take a break! Enjoy a mani-pedi, take a stroll with a friend, curl up with a book, or binge-watch your favorite show. **25**	Cook and prep as much as you can today so that tomorrow you can breathe easier. **26**
Start thinking Christmas! Gather the recipes you're using for holiday baking (page 80). **30**			

THURSDAY	FRIDAY	SATURDAY
		Invite friends and family for Thanksgiving. If guests are bringing a dish, make a note. Decide on the rest of the menu, and start a shopping list. **1**
Inventory your china, linens, flatware, and glasses. Place sticky notes on serving platters to note what will be served on each piece. **6**	Ask family and friends for gift ideas to get a jump start on your holiday shopping. **7**	Take stock of your pots, pans, and baking dishes. Buy or borrow any special kitchen equipment you might need to make meals. **8**
Clean the fridge. Dissolve 2 tablespoons of baking soda in 1 quart of warm water to wipe down the shelves. **13**	Shop for nonperishables and pantry staples. Check out bulk bins to save money on pricier items, like nuts and dried fruit. **14**	Give your house a top-to-bottom cleaning. Start in less-trafficked rooms, which aren't as likely to get messy. **15**
Planning to throw a Christmas cocktail party? Calendars fill up quickly, so aim to get your invites in the mail now. **20**	Preparing a frozen turkey? Calculate thawing time. Allow one day in the refrigerator for every 4 pounds. **21**	Make space in your coat closet, and tidy up the entry and public spaces of your home. **22**
Happy Thanksgiving! Accept help from guests who offer—they will feel good about pitching in, and you will have more time to relax and enjoy the day. **Thanksgiving 27**	Shoppers, start your engines—it's Black Friday! Visit *allyou.com* for great deals. **28**	Enjoy those yummy Thanksgiving leftovers! **29**

Centerpieces in Seconds

Use everyday items in creative ways for striking table displays.

- Arrange flowers in pitchers, creamers, and gravy boats and line them down the center of the table.

- Place votive candles and jingle bells in wineglasses, and display them on top of a mirrored place mat for reflective sparkle.

- Use a long fabric remnant as a table runner. Simply turn under and press the raw edges along the ends of the fabric.

- Fill small glass vases or jelly jars with candies in bright holiday colors. Hang candy canes on the rims of wine and martini glasses.

- Fill clear hurricanes or large vases with shiny ornaments. Scatter individual ornaments around the vases and down the middle of the table.

HOLIDAY HOTLINES

Use these toll-free numbers when you have last-minute food questions.

USDA Meat & Poultry Hotline:
1-888-674-6854

FDA Center for Food Safety:
1-888-723-3366

Butterball Turkey Talk Line:
1-800-BUTTERBALL

Butterball Turkey Text Line:
1-844-877-3456

Jennie-O Turkey Hotline:
1-800-TURKEYS

Ocean Spray Holiday Helpline:
1-800-662-3263

Fleischmann's Yeast Baker Hotline: 1-800-777-4959

December 2025 *daily to-dos:*

SUNDAY	MONDAY	TUESDAY	WEDNESDAY
	If you prefer to shop online for holiday gifts, start clicking for great Cyber Monday deals! **1**	Make a playlist of favorite holiday songs. It's never too early to get in the spirit and enjoy seasonal tunes. **2**	Organize gift wrap, cards, ribbons, tape, and scissors. Keep it all in a large tote so you can wrap gifts wherever you want. **3**
Find out if a local organization is hosting a food or gift drive. If you can, volunteer for a day or donate for those in need. **7**	Gather up unused gift cards and check expiration dates. Don't let those dollars go to waste. Add those savings to your gift-buying budget. **8**	Put kids to work making a garland of cranberries or popcorn using dental floss—it's strong, and its slippery coating speeds up stringing. Make extra popcorn for snacking! **9**	Pull out and test holiday string lights. Plug them into a timer. Your electric bill will thank you. **10**
Make gifts from the kitchen (page 158). Purchase jars, tins, or take-out boxes from the craft store to package treats for giving. **14**	Keep the Christmas tree fresh and hydrated. Top off the water reservoir every few days using a funnel so water won't spill near the electrical cords. **15**	Acknowledge those who brighten your day—a teacher, mail carrier, babysitter, or favorite colleague—with a small gift to show your appreciation. **16**	Check off your list! This is the last day to order gifts online before shipping prices jump with less than a week until Christmas. **17**
Winter Solstice. It's the first day of winter. After today, days will start getting longer again! **21**	Kick the holiday spirit into high gear with a classic film like *It's a Wonderful Life* or *A Christmas Story*. **22**	Wrap the last of your holiday gifts today so you don't have to stay up late on Christmas Eve! **23**	Gather loved ones for an elegant Christmas Eve dinner (page 66). **24**
Phone loved ones you didn't get to see over the holidays to catch up and let them know you're thinking of them. **28**	Head to the store today to return or exchange any gifts that weren't quite right before it's too late. **29**	Don't wait for resolutions. Get a jump on 2026 and get moving today. Take a walk, join a gym class, or enjoy a good stretch. **30**	Celebrate New Year's Eve with friends and loved ones, and toast the year ahead—and the wonders of this holiday season. **31**

THURSDAY	FRIDAY	SATURDAY
Get crafty today with our creative ideas for decorating with fruit (page 40). **4**	Make plans to host a good luck feast (page 90) to ring in the New Year. Keep it casual and text, call, or email your invitation. **5**	Send out those holiday cards today. The lines at the post office will only get longer. **6**
Trim the tree, hang those wreaths, display holiday cards, and dust off those Christmas knickknacks now so you can enjoy the display longer. **11**	Build a candy creation. Make a beautiful gingerbread house to display using one of the simple kits available online or at the grocery store. **12**	Set aside a couple of hours to wrap your holiday gifts. Beneath the tree, they add to the decor and anticipation. **13**
Bundle up and stroll the neighborhood after dinner with family and friends to enjoy the Christmas lights. **18**	Put your feet up. Enjoy a break from holiday prep and treat yourself to something you love or simply a long winter's nap. **19**	Call a local nursing home and arrange to visit residents who may be feeling lonely this time of year. **20**
Merry Christmas! Don't forget to charge your phone or camera so you can be sure to capture every wonderful moment. **25**	Take a break from cooking and indulge in all the tasty leftovers from your holiday dinner. **26**	Plan and prep for the New Year's feast (page 90). **27**

Place Card Panache

■ **Fanciful Forkful.** Enlist serving pieces as whimsical place cards. Fill a mint julep cup with moist florist foam and a small bundle of hypericum berries. Push the handle of a fork into the foam, and weave a place card between the tines (as shown).

■ **Personal Posy.** Write guests' names on rectangles of heavy paper. Punch near the edge of one short end. Just before the meal, slide short flower stems through the hole and prop atop dinner plates.

■ **Picture This.** Use mini picture frames as place cards that also serve as party favors. Inscribe names on paper, and slip them inside the frames.

■ **Pretty Pomander.** Greet dinner guests with initialed, clove-studded oranges. Use a pen to sketch an initial on each orange, and then press whole cloves into the orange following the marked letter. Let guests take home their fragrant pomanders, which should last about a week.

HOLIDAY PLANNER

Decorating Planner

Here's a list of details and finishing touches you can use to tailor a picture-perfect house this holiday season.

Decorative materials needed

FROM THE YARD ....

FROM AROUND THE HOUSE ....

....

FROM THE STORE ....

....

OTHER ....

Holiday decorations

FOR THE TABLE ....

....

FOR THE DOOR ....

....

FOR THE MANTEL ....

....

FOR THE STAIRCASE ....

....

OTHER ....

Create a Decorator's Toolkit

Our photo stylists guard their toolkits like the family jewels. A well-stocked kit means you have just what you need at the ready to get you through the holidays and beyond.

- ☐ Tools (hammer, screwdrivers, clamps)
- ☐ Nails, screws, S-hooks, U-pins, tacks
- ☐ Command strips and hooks
- ☐ Staple gun and staples
- ☐ Hot-glue gun and glue sticks
- ☐ Craft glue
- ☐ Super glue
- ☐ Clothespins
- ☐ Funnel
- ☐ Tape measure
- ☐ Twine
- ☐ Fishing line
- ☐ Green florists wire
- ☐ Sewing kit
- ☐ Lint roller
- ☐ Steamer or iron
- ☐ Paintbrushes (assorted)
- ☐ Scissors
- ☐ Florists snips
- ☐ Lighter
- ☐ Batteries (assorted)
- ☐ Fuses for string lights
- ☐ Scotch tape
- ☐ Double-sided tape
- ☐ Painters tape
- ☐ Museum Wax
- ☐ Putty
- ☐ Goo-Gone
- ☐ WD-40
- ☐ Window cleaner
- ☐ Furniture polish
- ☐ Touch-up paint
- ☐ Static duster
- ☐ Stain stick

How Lovely Are Your Branches!

For wreaths, garlands, trees, centerpieces, and more, enlist these eight types of greenery for lush holiday displays.

SILVER DOLLAR AND SEEDED EUCALYPTUS are fragrant choices with striking blue-gray leaves and tight berries that look more loose and modern than the usual conifer. Eucalyptus is great for flower arrangements because it has a long life when kept in a vase of water. It has a pleasing scent too.

CEDAR'S natural oils and striking leaf edges give branches staying power. With its dramatic draping effect, cedar looks great just about anywhere you choose to weave it in. Its lovely smell keeps moths at bay to boot.

BOXWOOD boasts tiny, roundish green leaves and a tight form that stays fresh-looking for weeks. Use it to line staircases, frame entryways, make wreaths, and more. It's a material that adds elegance to any holiday decor.

JUNIPER delivers fragrance, striking blue berries, and hardy leaves that hold up well whether used inside or out. Wear garden gloves when working with juniper to protect hands from its prickly foliage.

OLIVE BRANCHES lend a modern Mediterranean feel to arrangements with foliage that curls as it dries for an interesting effect. Mist it regularly with water to keep it looking fresh.

FIR BRANCHES are a gorgeous deep green with a dense habit that's a beloved holiday classic material for centerpieces, mantels, mailboxes, and swags for sconces and doors.

PINE has long, silky green needles and a refreshing, clean scent. It adds a gorgeous contrasting texture when tucked in to floral arrangements and mixed evergreen wreaths.

MAGNOLIA boasts big, sturdy, glossy-green leaves with velvety copper backs that lend a striking, natural palette to holiday decorating. If stored in a cool, dry place, magnolia wreaths and garlands can last for years.

Party Planner

Stay on top of your party plans with this time-saving menu organizer.

GUESTS	WHAT THEY'RE BRINGING	SERVING PIECES NEEDED
......	☐ appetizer ☐ beverage ☐ bread ☐ main dish ☐ side dish ☐ dessert	......
......	☐ appetizer ☐ beverage ☐ bread ☐ main dish ☐ side dish ☐ dessert	......
......	☐ appetizer ☐ beverage ☐ bread ☐ main dish ☐ side dish ☐ dessert	......
......	☐ appetizer ☐ beverage ☐ bread ☐ main dish ☐ side dish ☐ dessert	......
......	☐ appetizer ☐ beverage ☐ bread ☐ main dish ☐ side dish ☐ dessert	......
......	☐ appetizer ☐ beverage ☐ bread ☐ main dish ☐ side dish ☐ dessert	......
......	☐ appetizer ☐ beverage ☐ bread ☐ main dish ☐ side dish ☐ dessert	......
......	☐ appetizer ☐ beverage ☐ bread ☐ main dish ☐ side dish ☐ dessert	......
......	☐ appetizer ☐ beverage ☐ bread ☐ main dish ☐ side dish ☐ dessert	......
......	☐ appetizer ☐ beverage ☐ bread ☐ main dish ☐ side dish ☐ dessert	......
......	☐ appetizer ☐ beverage ☐ bread ☐ main dish ☐ side dish ☐ dessert	......
......	☐ appetizer ☐ beverage ☐ bread ☐ main dish ☐ side dish ☐ dessert	......
......	☐ appetizer ☐ beverage ☐ bread ☐ main dish ☐ side dish ☐ dessert	......
......	☐ appetizer ☐ beverage ☐ bread ☐ main dish ☐ side dish ☐ dessert	......
......	☐ appetizer ☐ beverage ☐ bread ☐ main dish ☐ side dish ☐ dessert	......
......	☐ appetizer ☐ beverage ☐ bread ☐ main dish ☐ side dish ☐ dessert	......
......	☐ appetizer ☐ beverage ☐ bread ☐ main dish ☐ side dish ☐ dessert	......

Party Guest List

Party To-Do List

Christmas Dinner Planner

Use this space to create a menu, to-do list, and guest list for your special holiday celebration.

Menu Ideas

Dinner To-Do List

Christmas Dinner Guest List

Pantry List

Grocery List

Gifts & Greetings

Keep up with family and friends' sizes, jot down gift ideas, and record purchases in this convenient chart. Also use it to keep track of addresses for your Christmas card list.

Gift List and Size Charts

	GIFT PURCHASED/MADE	SENT

....

jeans_____ shirt_____ sweater_____ jacket_____ shoes_____ belt_____
blouse_____ skirt_____ slacks_____ dress_____ suit_____ coat_____
pajamas_____ robe_____ hat_____ gloves_____ ring_____

jeans_____ shirt_____ sweater_____ jacket_____ shoes_____ belt_____
blouse_____ skirt_____ slacks_____ dress_____ suit_____ coat_____
pajamas_____ robe_____ hat_____ gloves_____ ring_____

jeans_____ shirt_____ sweater_____ jacket_____ shoes_____ belt_____
blouse_____ skirt_____ slacks_____ dress_____ suit_____ coat_____
pajamas_____ robe_____ hat_____ gloves_____ ring_____

jeans_____ shirt_____ sweater_____ jacket_____ shoes_____ belt_____
blouse_____ skirt_____ slacks_____ dress_____ suit_____ coat_____
pajamas_____ robe_____ hat_____ gloves_____ ring_____

jeans_____ shirt_____ sweater_____ jacket_____ shoes_____ belt_____
blouse_____ skirt_____ slacks_____ dress_____ suit_____ coat_____
pajamas_____ robe_____ hat_____ gloves_____ ring_____

jeans_____ shirt_____ sweater_____ jacket_____ shoes_____ belt_____
blouse_____ skirt_____ slacks_____ dress_____ suit_____ coat_____
pajamas_____ robe_____ hat_____ gloves_____ ring_____

jeans_____ shirt_____ sweater_____ jacket_____ shoes_____ belt_____
blouse_____ skirt_____ slacks_____ dress_____ suit_____ coat_____
pajamas_____ robe_____ hat_____ gloves_____ ring_____

Christmas Card List

NAME   ADDRESS   SENT

Holiday Memories

Hold on to priceless Christmas memories forever with handwritten recollections of this season's magical moments.

Treasured Traditions

Keep track of your family's favorite holiday customs and pastimes on these lines.

....
....
....
....
....
....
....
....
....
....
....
....
....
....

Special Holiday Activities

What holiday events do you look forward to year after year? Write them down here.

....
....
....
....
....
....
....
....
....
....
....

Holiday Visits and Visitors

Keep a list of this year's holiday visitors. Jot down friend and family news as well.

....
....
....
....
....
....
....
....
....
....
....
....
....
....
....
....
....
....
....
....
....
....
....
....
....
....
....
....

This Year's Favorite Recipes

APPETIZERS AND BEVERAGES

....
....
....
....
....

ENTRÉES

....
....
....
....

SIDES AND SALADS

....
....
....
....

COOKIES AND CANDIES

....
....
....
....

DESSERTS

....
....
....
....

Looking Ahead

Holiday Wrap-Up

Use this checklist to record thank-you notes sent for holiday gifts and hospitality.

NAME	GIFT AND/OR EVENT	NOTE SENT
		☐
		☐
		☐
		☐
		☐
		☐
		☐
		☐
		☐
		☐
		☐
		☐
		☐

Notes for Next Year

Write down your ideas for Christmas 2026 on the lines below.

HOLIDAY PLANNER